Leading Your Ministry to Financial Health

By

William F. Johnson

Leading Your Church to Financial Health

By

William F. Johnson

ISBN-13: 978-0615949161

Published by

Aslan Press

PO Box 176

Mendenhall, MS 39114

www.aslanpress.com

© 2014

Dedication

This book is dedicated to my wife Rita, for her love and support throughout our journey together as we try to follow the Lord where ever He leads us.

Forward:

How do ministries become healthier financially?

A mentor of mine introduced me to Biblical principles that answer this question. That mentor is Bill Johnson, my friend and former Pastor. Although written for pastors and ministry leaders, this book provides a success model for all God centered businesses and skills that can be used in every day life.

In 1995 my family was attending a church when Bill and Rita were called to be the pastors. The church was hurting and discouraged. They ministered, love and taught us. Over the next several years the church became a healthy, loving, and a purposeful church. This book includes many of the Biblical based principles of ministry and leadership they used to disciple us and empowered us to participate in setting ministry goals. We were encouraged to be involved. No one's idea was summarily dismissed or tabled. Bill made you feel good even if our idea was not.

The church went out into the community with random acts of kindness, doing yard work for people that were less able, giving away free soft drinks at street corners, handing out light bulbs and school supplies in disadvantaged neighborhoods. Our Minden Church began to experience more unity than I have ever seen in any church of which we have been a part. We had a strong, functioning leadership team in place.

Bill led the Community Ministerial Alliance skillfully through ethnic lines.

When Bill and Rita decided to retire, they appointed interim leaders from the existing body and moved back to Mississippi. While grieving over our loss we began to adjust and the church continued to flourish under its lay leadership team. The training provided by Bill and Rita was tested as we learned quickly the tasks of church leadership. That training made a big difference as the church continued for nearly two years with lay leadership. This book brings me back to that time and value of that training.

I was blessed to retire from a family operated business that incorporated the values described in this book. I was a witness to how God provided for this company. The owners, the leadership team, and the employees all held integrity and stewardship of the company resources as core values. Employees were treated as valuable assets and shared the company values. Giving to churches, seminaries, children's homes, and colleges was a priority. The company was blessed with excellent talent and business opportunities for developing natural resources. We participated in some of the very best projects in partnership with some of the top companies in our industry. God blessed this company as they were able to bless Christian ministries.

Bill traveled a very diverse path leading to his pastoral and teaching ministries. After graduating from Georgia Tech, Bill served as commanding officer of the Seventh US Army Data Communications Network in Europe, where his leadership opportunities began. Back in civilian life, from engineering, he moved into marketing and then executive management, often opening up new markets and new facilities. His teaching and curricula development was honed as he developed training classes for the military and other government agencies.

Shortly after meeting his wife, Rita, Bill began to depend upon the Lord for his life and career. When offered an opportunity to start a new division of an engineering services company in San Diego they entered into a time of prayer and felt the Lord was leading them to make the move from Mississippi. Several years later that organization had become a multimillion dollar international organization, but God was calling them in a different direction.

The Johnson's activities in the church were also growing rapidly. At the peak of his secular career, the Lord called Bill into full time ministry - an offer he could not refuse. Bill left his top floor, corner office, impressive title, and big salary to accept part time employment and full time ministry. This entailed and a move to the Pacific Northwest. Together they led many renewal events and Bill was assisting churches as a consultant on church effectiveness throughout the eleven western states. When Bill graduated from Fuller Theological Seminary they continued their teaching but added church planting to their activities.

Bill and Rita now lead Aslan Ministries which provides support and counsel to pastors and church leaders. Aslan develops resources and provides training tools in the areas of ministry and leadership development.

This book is published as a guide to successful leadership and a mentoring tool for ministry leaders. It provides a Scriptural pathway to a financially sound and successful ministry. It explains how a leader can develop a mentoring leadership style. One foundational topic is devoted to developing a unified purpose within the ministry by building relationships and identifying Spiritual Gifting.

Ronnie E. Bounds, Jr. Encourager, Equipper, Financial Analyst, Retired Oil Company Executive

1. The Problem

The finance committee in a local church was meeting to consider the budget for the coming year. Trustees presented estimates for utilities and maintenance. Utilities are to be increased over the previous year by ten percent. Expenses for buildings and grounds include repairs to the roof and air conditioning system. The trustee's budget was approved with no changes. There would be no change to salaries for the pastor and staff. The Christian education budget was increased as a result of curricula costs. When compared with the projected income, there was little left for outreach, missions, and local ministry. Does this sound familiar to you?

If this were your church, what would you do? If this is your church, what will you do? This situation is faced by thousands of churches and non-profit ministries throughout the world. In fact it is rare for ministries to have all of the resources they need to accomplish their mission. It is a problem but it is often the way we in the Christian community operate. After spending half of my adult life in the business arena, I can look at the church and say, "This is no way to run a business." Now, after spending the second half of my adult life leading churches and ministries I have to say, "Churches and Christian ministries are not businesses and should not be run in the same way businesses are run." As much as business leaders profess a social conscience, their organizations are established to make a profit for the owners or stock holders. On the other hand, churches and ministries exist for expanding the kingdom of God. They exist to take the Good News to lost and hurting people. The church has only one stockholder who needs to be satisfied. That is the head of the church, our Lord Jesus Christ.[1] Satisfying Him includes being good stewards of His resources. Sound financial practices are important not because they are good for business, but because they are directed by scripture. While we are not of this world, we do live in this world and influenced by what goes on in the world around us. The church cannot function isolated from the world; although there are some who feel otherwise.

Being in the world, we experience situations taking place in the world today. For the past several years the unemployment rate in the US and around the world has maintained levels usually associated with recession if not depression. We have had several years of economic down-turn. The Barna Group issued their annual report on the impact of the economy on Church Giving in July of 2012.

> *The financial problems afflicting economies around the world has influenced Americans' generosity: 41% of all U.S. adults say they have reduced giving to non-profit organizations as a result of the poor economy in the last three months. This was roughly on par with the level of charitable reduction discovered in 2011 (39%).*
>
> *As for giving to churches, Americans are increasingly likely to cut back on donations to congregations and houses of worship. In the current study, one-third of Americans (34%) have dropped*

---

[1] Colossians 1:18

the amount donated to churches in the last three months. This is the highest the indicator has been since the tracking began in 2008.

Furthermore, 11% of Americans say they have completely dropped all giving to churches in recent months, also the highest it has been in the four waves of tracking conducted by Barna. In November of 2008, 4% had cut church giving entirely, but 7% had done so in April 2011.

Difficult economic times cause individuals and foundations to re-evaluate their charitable giving. As a result, leaders of organizations that rely on outside financial support face the increasingly difficult task of justifying their existence. Service organizations, churches, and ministries often struggle to maintain their existence in times of economic uncertainty. Those that have money in difficult times, become more particular where they give. When family income dwindles, with loss of a job or cut back in salary, charitable giving is reduced or totally discontinued. Competition for charitable contributions becomes intense. I have found that there is always plenty of money and resources if people can see how they can become a part of something exciting.

Statistical information is a good barometer for understanding what is happening across a large segment of the population, but it does not account for individual ministries which are running counter to the trend and are thriving even in this difficult economy. Why are they not feeling the economic crunch?

While major mainline denominations continue to lose membership, other faith based, Christian entities are financially solid and growing at unprecedented rates.

The problem is not the lack of resources. Our God does not need for money. God does not need our money, He is wealthy. He owns the cattle on a thousand hills; every animal in the forest is His.[2] God's resources here on earth are often in the hands of His people.

If the issue is not lack of resources, what is the problem? There are at least three possible answers; lack of a large enough vision, lack of God's support, or failure to communicate.

---

[2] Psalm 50:9-10

2. Leaders dilemma

It is the leader's role to make sure that the organization is healthy and continues to serve the purpose for which it was established. This usually involves the gathering and disbursing of resources. Financial resources are necessary for most ministries. How should a leader proceed in seeking financial support? What is a leader to do when the finances are not available? If the finances are not able to support the ministry there are three possibilities; lack of vision, God is not involved, or poor the leader's inability to communicate.

At a community gathering early in my ministry, I was asked to take the offering for a local outreach ministry. The cause was worthy and the need was great. My appeal was strong, emotional, and effective. The offering exceeded all expectations. The ministry received more than twice the amount they had ever received at any previous gathering. But something was wrong, why did I feel so bad? The objective had been achieved, but instead of self-satisfaction there was sadness. It was not until the next day that I realized why I felt so strange. The Holy Spirit revealed to me that people gave for the wrong reasons. They had been manipulated. My methods of persuasion took away their joy in giving. Yes, it was a worthy cause. Yes, they wanted to give, but my actions were offensive. Nobody likes to be manipulated into giving. Rather than trusting God to speak into the hearts of the audience, I used worldly techniques to accomplish the task at hand. Later I had to ask myself, "Was my presentation designed to raise money for the needs of the ministry or was it to impress my peers?"

This long ago incident showed me something about myself which was not pleasant to see; manipulation came easy. Consequently, I went to the opposite extreme and became hesitant to ask for money for fear of offending or embarrassing someone. Obviously my attitude over financial issues needed correcting. God began to put me into leadership roles in churches and ministries where financial issues required biblical solutions. The Christian walk is full of testing, but we can never flunk God's test. If we fail to pass, He allows us to retake the exam. Some of us retake the same test hundreds of times before we get it right. The Israelites spent forty years walking around in the desert until they were ready to cross into the Promised Land. Here is a good point to remember: if you seem to be going around in circles and not making progress, in whatever you are trying to accomplish, the Lord may be trying to teach you something.

What is appropriate in attracting the resources required to fulfill God's call? Most ministry leaders are like I was after my manipulation experience; they do not like to ask for money. Yet every ministry needs resources in order to fulfill its purpose. The subject is not taught in seminaries, at least not in mine. Yet each church or ministry requires financial support so they can devote their time to building God's kingdom. Each leader must come face to face with the difficult task of raising funds to continue the ministry.

In the area of raising financial support, leaders often fall into two distinct and polar opposite traps - manipulation or passivity. The manipulation trap relies on worldly techniques such as, persuasion, guilt, and emotion.

Ministries are normally started with a specific God-given purpose. It may be to reach lost people with the Gospel or improve the conditions of the least of God's children. Often as the ministry grows, something begins to happen. The organization becomes more important than ministry to the people. As a result, God's blessing is removed. The organization now must resort to worldly techniques in order to raise the money needed for the organization to survive. This may occur in any church or ministry organization when the survival of that organization becomes more important than God's call. This is called institutionalization. The passivity trap results from a leader's fear of talking about finances. This type of leader may be sensitive to the complaint that all the church does is ask for money. He may be more fearful of the people than he is of God. Another reason the leader may be passive is an overly spiritualized approach. "God knows our need and he will provide." God will provide, but He usually uses people as His instrument.

Universities, large ministries, political groups, and relief organizations employ a full time staff whose single responsibility is raising money and developing a support base. But, most church leaders, ministry leaders and missionaries will have to do their own fund raising. Their gifts and graces are generally limited to their particular areas of ministry and not to raising support. Most missionary sending organizations require the missionaries to return home for a time to raise support. Instead of coming home for rest and recuperation they require, they must travel from place to place raising financial support. As a result the business of ministry can get in the way of serving Jesus.

3. The Leader

John Wimber, the late leader of the Vineyard movement often said, "If you want to know whether you are a leader, look behind you, and see if there is anyone following you." You can learn all about leadership, you can think you are a good leader, but the proof is in who is following you. Leaders lead and there are people who are following. Followers imitate the leader. Wimber had a beard and wore Hawaiian shirts and sneakers. It is amazing how many pastors in the Vineyard movement, even today, have beards and wear Hawaiian shirts and sneakers.

In the same way, the people following you will act and do many of the same things you do. If you are reaching out to the unchurched in your community, they will also. If you are generous with your resources they will copy you. If you are doing great things and no one is with you, you are probably not leading them. Similarly, if you are not getting outside of the church walls, your people will probably not be reaching out. A church planter will spend much of his time gathering people. As the church grows, he may spend more time on other things and ignore outreach. When the leader does not go out, his followers will also stay in. The bottom line to this is if you want your people to change, you will have to change yourself. If they are not following, find out why you are not leading and work on becoming a better leader.

So what makes a leader? Popular author and leadership guru, John C. Maxwell,[3] often notes that, "Leadership is influence." If we want to be a better leader then we must gain influence. Adam Grant in his recent book "Give and Take, A Revolutionary Approach to Success" suggests there are two ways to gain influence:

> *Research suggests that there are two fundamental paths to influence: dominance and prestige. When we establish dominance, we gain influence because others see us as strong, powerful, and authoritative. When we earn prestige, we become influential because others respect and admire us.*[4]

According to Grant, those who would dominate will raise their voices, promote their accomplishments, and use power displaying body language. While dominance may have an immediate impact on people, it is usually short lived. When taking my first public offering I resorted to dominance. Those who gain influence through prestige communicate less powerfully and often show vulnerability. Prestige can be gained through the character of the leader; a personal identity, a Godly self confidence, purpose, integrity, and a servant attitude. Grant puts people into three categories; givers, takers, and matchers. Takers look for what they can get for themselves and will often resort to dominance to get what they want.

---

[3] www.johnmaxwell.com

[4] Grant Ph.D., Adam M. (2013-04-09). Give and Take: A Revolutionary Approach to Success (p. 130). Penguin Group US.

Givers seek to help others, having a servant heart. Matchers feel the need to reciprocate, they keep score, and they will often give something in order to get something in return. An analysis of the variety of leadership styles and techniques is beyond the scope of this book, but it is important to realize that effective leaders understand the needs of their followers and adapt their methods accordingly.

Christian leaders are called to serve God and those who they lead. They are to be servant leaders, building prestige by helping those they lead become successful. Our model for leadership has to be Jesus. A review of His leadership methods should be our guide. Jesus' deity is fundamental to the Christian religion. As God, He could have come into this world as a conqueror. He could have led by domination, yet He chose to enter this world as we do, through the womb of a woman. He could have gathered His disciples by drafting them into His army and using His power to force them to follow. Yet He just called to them, "Come, follow me," and they left their family and positions and followed Him. Jesus could have used "dominance" to influence people but He chose to use "prestige."

How can we develop "prestige? Follow the model of Jesus. Jesus walked with an identity, self confidence, purpose, integrity, and a servant attitude.

Identity

Leaders must walk in the knowledge of who they are. You can not develop prestige if you are trying to be someone else. You have to know who you are and what you were created to be. Many of us grow up confused about our identity, but not Jesus.

At the age of twelve while His family was on the way home from Jerusalem, unbeknownst to them, Jesus had stayed behind in the temple. When they scolded Him for being away, He responded. "I must be about my Father's business."[5] Jesus knew at that age why He was here and what He was to accomplish. We each must understand what we are here for and what we are to accomplish. It does not depend upon a position or title that we have been given; it depends upon God's sovereign call. Too often we try to be someone we are not. Others may try to give us our identity, but that identity comes from God alone. C. S. Lewis writes in "Mere Christianity,"

> *"Your real, new self (which is Christ's and also yours, and yours just because it is His) will not come as long as you are looking for it. It will come when you are looking for Him."*

Just before Jesus met His most difficult challenges, the temptation by Satan and the cross, God the Father appeared and spoke, "This is my beloved Son..." Each time Jesus was reminded of His identity.

---

[5] Luke 2:49

When we understand our identity in Christ, we can have peace with ourselves and will be able to handle criticism and failure without self pity and defensiveness. Understanding our identity will lead us to our purpose. Know yourself; know your relationship with God. Spend time in prayer. Know what God is calling you to become.

Self Confidence

As leaders we need to walk with a Godly self confidence. Too often we fear failure so much that we are frozen in place and cannot take the next step. We must eliminate our fears of failure, rejection, and/or humiliation. Good people will only condemn others for not trying.

They will not condemn someone for trying and failing. Home run hitters in baseball strike out more often than they hit homeruns. The baseball legend Babe Ruth set the record for the most home runs in a season and also the most strikeouts in a season.

Ruth's record for strikeouts was broken by Sammy Sosa who also broke Ruth's homerun record by hitting sixty two homers. Most people who have accomplished great things have also failed a number of times. This is true not only in sports but also in business and the church. We do not have to fear failure but we should develop a healthy fear of God. It is easy to fall into the trap of trying to please people, but we are to be God pleasers. Do not be afraid of what others might think. We should attempt something so great for God that it is doomed to fail unless God is in it. It is far better to attempt something great and fail than to attempt nothing and succeed.

The cowardly, find their place in the lake of fire along with the unbelieving, the vile, the murderers, the sexually immoral, those who practice magic arts, the idolaters and all liars....[6] Accept where God has put you and get to work. Be thankful for your positive strengths.

Use them, make the best of them. Believe in the importance of your mission. Otherwise you will be just playing church. Have Faith for the future. Expect success. If God has called you he will build His church to be what He wants it to be.

Purpose

Leaders must walk with purpose. Throughout all of His life here on earth, Jesus understood and knew His purpose. He revealed God the Father, lived a sinless life and died on the cross to reconcile us to God. We will never have peace in our lives until we understand our unique individual purpose. Our purpose will be fired by a passion which is strong enough for us to sacrifice other things in order to achieve it. Our purpose cannot be based alone upon the needs around us, but on Jesus' call. Our unique purpose must come from God. Jesus came into the world to show us the Father and through His death on the cross provided us a means to relate intimately with God.

---

[6] Revelation 21:8

There is so much need in the world today that most of us fall into one of two possible groupings; those who try to do everything and those who see the task as being too huge so they give up before they start. The former category leads to early burn out while the latter group sits back and does nothing. We must find out what our particular piece of the task is and do that. To identify our purpose we must seek God, consult respected spiritual leaders, and search scripture.[7] Then we will have peace.

Integrity

Leaders must above all else have integrity. Jesus had ultimate integrity. He was without sin. That is why He could fulfill our need for a sacrifice.[8]

When we speak, we must speak the truth without exaggeration. When we make promises, we must follow through. When we speak we must be accurate and avoid exaggeration. We must be honest and careful with money, both ours and the ministry's. We must be morally sound and we must live what we preach. There seems to be a real lack of character and integrity in our nation and the world today. The lack of integrity in our leaders screams at us daily from the news media as another church leader, politician, or business executive is caught lying, stealing, or being caught in immorality.

---

[7] Resources in identifying your purpose can be found at www.aslanministries.org

[8] Hebrews 9:11-15

Church and ministry leaders must be beyond reproach in dealing with God's ministries.

> *James 3:13-18 Who is wise and understanding among you? Let him show it by his good life, by deeds done in the humility that comes from wisdom. [14]But if you harbor bitter envy and selfish ambition in your hearts, do not boast about it or deny the truth. [15]Such "wisdom" does not come down from heaven but is earthly, unspiritual, of the devil. [16]For where you have envy and selfish ambition, there you find disorder and every evil practice. [17]But the wisdom that comes from heaven is first of all pure; then peace-loving, considerate, submissive, full of mercy and good fruit, impartial and sincere. [18]Peacemakers who sow in peace raise a harvest of righteousness.*

Servant-hood

Leaders must walk in servant-hood. Jesus was the embodiment of a servant leader. Not only did He willingly go to the cross, but in His daily interaction with His followers, He put them ahead of His own agenda. On His way to heal the daughter of the ruler of the synagogue, He stopped to address the woman who had touched Him.[9]

---

[9] Mark 5:21-34

Servant leaders are givers, who help others become successful. In the past, church growth experts emphasized the need for the senior leader to delegate. They used the analogy of a rancher versus a farmer. The farmer could handle a small farm while the rancher could handle a larger spread by delegating authority and responsibility to others.

This pattern often failed because the rancher became threatened by the success of an underling. We have heard from many leaders, primarily in the church, who have had bad experiences in the delegation of tasks and responsibility. Even though you delegate, the person performing the task has to be held accountable.

Rather than be threatened the true servant leader wants to see others become successful. Jesus told His disciples; whoever believes in Him will do greater things than Jesus.[10] The role of a servant leader is to help his or her followers become all that God created them to be.

Once you have the reputation of being the type of person others want to emulate it is important to maintain that position. In order to have authority over people, leaders must also be under authority. All authority is delegated from God. If you as a leader cannot be under authority, you cannot be trusted with authority. If you have unresolved hurts from someone who is over you, you end up doing to others what has been done to you. If you relate well to those over you, you will be able to serve those under you.

---

[10] John 14:12

Keep righteous relationships with other people. Do not get over fatigued. Fatigue will cause you to not listen, jump to conclusions, and do and say things you should not. Watch what you say. Leaders are more accountable[11]. Words have a tremendous effect on others. Do not criticize others behind their back. Watch out for promises you cannot keep. Private conversations must be kept private. Respect the rights and emotions of others.

Servant leaders walk in humility; they are honest about their weaknesses and limitations. Be a learner; do not be afraid to say, "I don't know." Change your mind once in awhile. Allow others to change your mind once in a while. Ask for help and advice once in awhile and when you are wrong, repent quickly.

---

[11] James 3:1

4. Anatomy of a Giver

One man gives freely, yet gains even more; another withholds unduly, but comes to poverty. A generous man will prosper; he who refreshes others will himself be refreshed. [Proverbs 11:24-25 (NIV)]

A tired and unkempt lady struggled with her overloaded grocery cart as she exited Albertson's grocery in Federal Way, Washington. The surface of the parking lot shimmered with radiant waves of heat. It was one of those rare hot days. Sweat was dripped from her forehead as she was approached by a man holding a frosty can of a popular cola. She received it indifferently laying on top of the heaping cart. When she got to her car, she placed the drink on the car's roof and began to load the groceries.

The trunk was not large enough to stow everything so she placed some in the back seat. As she got into the car she grabbed the cola and noticed a card under the pop top tab. Now sitting behind the wheel, she picked up the card and read,

> *"You looked too thirsty to pass up.*
> *We hope this little gift*
> *brings a little light into your day.*
> *It is our way of telling you,*
> *'GOD LOVES YOU,*
> *No strings attached."*

Suddenly tears mixed with sweat and mascara ran down her face. Getting out of her car, holding the card high above her head, she walked back to the man who had handed her the drink. The tears flowed freely as she thanked the man and told him her story.

"It was a year ago that my child died. I was so angry with God that I tried to shut Him out of my life. But recently I have felt that He was reaching out to me and that I needed to start back to church. This card and your gift have confirmed that. You do not know how much this has meant to me. Thank you."

This episode is just one of many that we experienced in taking the church into the streets to reach people with the love of God. Servant Evangelism, pioneered by Steve Sjogren at his church in Cincinnati, is a powerful witness of God's love to hurting people. Random acts of kindness helped his church grow to several thousand. When churches actively show God's love to hurting and desperate people in simple practical ways, it changes the church. Many churches do simple things like giving away; light bulbs, batteries for smoke detectors, free car washes, coffee, and cocoa. Churches that have adopted this model of outreach affect their communities and best of all it stimulates their own congregations. Most realize numerical growth in their church but not for the reason you might imagine. Few of the people served become church members, but the lives of servants are transformed. Stepping out of their comfort zones, they return telling stories, like the one cited above, and share of how God moved. The old adage, "It is more blessed to give than to receive," certainly holds true.

A pastor in Colorado was having a difficult time motivating his congregation to give cheerfully and fully to the work of the church. As he discussed this with others at the local ministerial association, another pastor gave a hearty. "Amen." It seems this other pastor was having serious problems. His church was being evicted and they did not have the money to move or make a down payment on another facility. As the first pastor prayed about the situation of the second pastor, an idea began to formulate in his heart. The next Sunday as he took the offering he explained, "Today's entire offering will be special. We will be giving it all to another church who has lost their lease and needs to get into another facility. They do not have the money to move. Please give generously."

The resulting offering was amazing. It was the largest offering the church had ever received. The money was given to the needy church that was then able to find a new facility. Interestingly, the giving church's offerings continued at the new giving level.

Similarly, a church near New Orleans gave their entire offering one Sunday to another church that had a building program. Both churches benefited as the giving church realized an increase in its giving. A generous man will prosper; he who refreshes others will himself be refreshed.[12]

---

[12] Proverbs 11:25

Adam Grant[13] writes that "givers" give more than they get, while "takers" get more than they give. Takers in a business setting appear to be stronger and are more often noticed when it is time for promotion. "Matchers" operate on the concept of fairness. They believe in reciprocity, "You do this for me and I will do that for you." One of the interesting things we found in giving away free items is there are some people who cannot receive something without trying to give something in return. These are the "Matchers." When doing free car washing or other good deeds, we notice that the recipients often want to give something in return. This gives us a perfect opening for sharing how God's love comes to us free with no strings attached.

Grant estimates there to be about fifteen percent of the general population are givers and my experience indicates a like percentage in the church. "Takers" in the church are those who feel they must be served. They come to the worship service and expect to be entertained. They complain that their needs are not being met.

There are pastors and leaders who are "takers," contrary to the model of Jesus' ministry while He was here on earth. Jesus did not come to be served but to serve.[14]

When the disciples argued as to who would be the greatest, Jesus instructed them that he who served, was the greatest.[15] Everyone in the church is called into service.

---

[13] Grant Ph.D., Adam M. (2013-04-09). Give And Take: A Revolutionary Approach To Success. Penguin Group Us.

[14] Matthew 10:28; Mark 10:25

Givers are the ones who serve other's interests before their own. All believers are called to give of our time, energy, and resources to support the growth of God's kingdom. The Bible teaches that all are to give freely[16]. But there is a special category of individual in the church who has been given a special grace from God to give more fully than others. Romans chapter twelve speaks of seven specific gifts of grace that are called motivational gifts. They are individually given to people within the church to aid the church in fulfilling its specific call.

I believe that God has placed people, in every church body, with the appropriate gift mix for that church to thrive. When a person operates in his or her particular gift mix, he or she excels in that area of activity.

One of those graces is the gift of generosity or giving. It is a good idea for each church to help their congregation to identify their giftedness so they will then be more effectively used in the church.[17]

The gift of giving is not restricted to the wealthy. The Macedonian church gave out of its poverty,[18] and Jesus praised the widow who only gave a mite.[19]

---

[15] Matthew 23:11; Mark 9:34-36

[16] Matthew 6:1-4; 2 Corinthians 9:6-7;

[17] A Gift Assessment can be downloaded free from www.aslanministries.org and selecting spiritual gifts from the menu.

[18] 2 Corinthians 8:1-2

[19] Mark 12:41-44

In scripture we find at least five areas of giving: Sharing material goods such as food, clothing, and shelter;[20] sharing of spiritual things;[21] sharing the Gospel;[22] sharing of one's self;[23] and sharing of finances.[24] Those with the gift of giving often find that making money is not difficult. The difficult thing is to know what to do with what resources the giver receives. It is a great responsibility to have the gift of giving. God provides givers with resources in order to finance the growth of His kingdom a giver can get into trouble when he assumes the resources he has are his own. It gets back to the ownership issue. Givers who begin to use God's resources for personal use rather than ministry often are hit with unforeseen expenses. On the other hand we know of people who had well over one hundred thousand miles on a set of tires and over two hundred thousand miles on a set of sparkplugs and no tune up. The ancient Israelites wandered in the desert for forty years and their shoes did not wear out.

The gift of giving is the Holy Spirit motivating believers to take that which they have, give it to support God's servants, freeing them to do the ministry to which God has called them.

---

[20] Luke 3:11; 1Kings 17:7-16

[21] Romans 1:11

[22] 1Thesalonians 2:8; John 20:31

[23] Acts 9:36-39

[24] Acts 4:37; Philippians 4:10-19

Givers have a keen discernment about wise investments and have the ability to make money and accumulate assets. A Giver undergirds and supports the ministry of others, which means he puts his trust in his fellow men and their particular ministries. A Giver has the ability to test people's faithfulness and wisdom in how they use the gifts, and wants to be a part of the ministry that he supports. A Giver is discerning about the ministries others may propose to him to support. In fact it may appear that he knows in advance which ministries will succeed and which will fail. A Giver is motivated to give at the Lord's prompting rather than give based upon human appeals. He absolutely refuses to be pressured into giving. In fact the surest way to turn him off is to pressure him. At this time some may think him selfish when in truth the opposite is true. A Giver often uses his or her giving to motivate others to give to the same cause. A Giver likes to give quietly and avoids publicity. A Giver wants to be led by God in his or her giving. His greatest joy then comes from learning that his gift is an answer to prayer or is confirmed by official action of those God has placed in authority in the church.

Stuff is not important to givers and they are not concerned about status. They have a tendency to practice personal frugality and are content with the bare necessities.

Our son, Kevin is a giver. When he was barely in high school Rita bought him a red, Arnold Palmer sports coat to wear to a funeral.

A year later he was going to a dance and Rita suggested he wear the red sports coat. Kevin explained that he no longer had it. A friend needed a coat, so Kevin gave it to him. To Kevin, a giver, it made perfect sense. To his mother, it was irresponsible. Givers normally are not attached to things.

Givers receive so many appeals and requests for money that their natural inclination is to say "no" when offered an opportunity to give. It upsets a giver to see others waste money, because they are able to see how that money could be used for ministry.

There are some negative issues which may occur when a Giver does not allow the Holy Spirit to lead. Often a giver, realizing that money can corrupt, may become too frugal with his or her own family. Since givers do not need much, they do not understand why other family members need more. They may fail to discern and follow God's prompting on giving. They may begin to judge rather than give advice to those who misuse funds. They may try to control people or ministries with their gifts. They may corrupt people by giving too much. They also may become "cause" oriented rather than "people" oriented and invest in projects which build institutions rather than benefitting people's lives.

> *2CO 9:6 "Remember this: Whoever sows sparingly will also reap sparingly, and whoever sows generously will also reap generously. Each man should give what he has decided in his heart to give, not reluctantly or under compulsion, for God loves a cheerful giver."*

There is a difference between someone who is obedient to God and gives and someone who is a cheerful giver. The cheerful giver is submitted to God.

5. Stewardship

In the church we have certain words that we hesitate to speak aloud: There is the "E" word, "Evangelism." Some people have that terrifying image of confronting someone on the street and asking, "Are you saved?" But also there is the dreaded "S" word, "Stewardship." We just do not want to talk about money! It feels like an invasion of someone's privacy.

For a few years into my pastoral ministry I avoided preaching on stewardship and giving. It was an over-reaction to my manipulating experience and a reaction to television evangelists. Then the pastor of a neighboring church asked me to be the keynote speaker at his church's annual stewardship campaign. Thanking him for the honor, but offering him an out, I explained, "I haven't preached about money for years." My friend responded, "But, your church is growing and your finances do not seem to be a problem. Maybe you could help us learn to give more like your church." When he put it that way, I could not refuse.

When we arrived at this particular church there were a number of problems. The church was in debt and current income was not meeting fixed needs. The founding pastor had left suddenly and people were confused. After a short time things had begun to change and now, after a few years, we were financially sound with a congregation growing numerically and spiritually.

Before entering ministry my experience had been in corporate leadership. Starting with a small engineering firm, we grew to a multi-million dollar international organization. Raising money had never been a serious concern. In ministry things changed. We no longer had employees and customers; we now had people with needs, volunteers, and supporters. It is important for all believers to understand God's principles on the stewardship of His resources, and as a leader, you have a responsibility to teach on stewardship. Stewardship is the proper management of your life in order to enhance the kingdom of God. Christians cannot grow to maturity until their hearts and minds are conformed to Scripture regarding the use of their resources.

> *"If a person gets his/her attitude toward money straight," it will help straighten out almost every other area in his/her life." Billy Graham*

> *"Every Christian needs two conversions, one for his soul and the other for his pocketbook." Martin Luther*

Jesus taught about money and stewardship in sixteen of His thirty eight parables. A tenth of the verses in the Gospels refer in part to financial matters. The Bible contains five hundred verses on prayer, less on faith, but there are over two thousand verses devoted to money and possessions. Paul warns leaders that wealth has an addictive effect on believers.[25]

The most fundamental issue regarding finances in the Bible is the issue of ownership - who owns our possessions?[26] Jesus used parables to teach basic truths about the Kingdom of God.

---

[25] 1 Timothy6:9-10, 6:17

[26] Matthew 25:14-30

Several parables describe a king or merchant entrusting his possessions to servants. Then he leaves the country for a time. When He returns home he determines how well the servants behaved. In the parable of the Talents, a man left three servants large amounts of money (talents). Then he went on a journey. The first two servants invested their master's talents wisely and doubled his money. Upon his return, the master praised the two servants and invited them to share in his happiness. The third servant, however, hid the master's money and earned nothing in his absence. The master was angry with him.

The parable of the talents reinforces Christ's exhortation that we be watchful in view of the unknown hour of His return, it teaches that all we have is owned by God, our life, family, our next breath , and all of our material possessions. The idea that we possess anything is a deception.

Through God's grace He provides us all we have. But we do not own any of it. We are merely stewards of His wealth, both the rich and the poor die, and they each leave this world as they carne into it – naked.[27] But like the servants in the parable of the Talents, we are entrusted with much; we are stewards of God's possessions.

Stewards manage another's property. They are accountable to fulfill the wishes of the owner. We have been redeemed at the cross, and our entire lives were purchased with the precious blood of Christ.

---

[27] Psalm 49:10; 1 Timothy 6:7

God now rightfully possesses the title deed to our souls, bodies, our aspirations, and our bank accounts. If we, as believers, understand that God is the owner of everything in our lives, then we can share in God's abundance.

In the Sermon on the Mount, Jesus spoke directly to the rivalry between money and heaven. A bumper sticker reads "he who dies with the most toys wins." That is not what Jesus taught.[28] Woody Allen once remarked, "Money is better than poverty, if only for financial reasons." But what are those financial reasons? The world says that money buys security, freedom, power, identity, pleasure, and happiness. In effect, Jesus says, "That may be true, but only for the moment. A day is coming when you can't take it with you." Money cannot make anyone rich in the things that count for eternity. Nothing of God's is obtainable by money.

When Simon the sorcerer saw the Holy Spirit come on people as Peter laid hands on them, he wanted to buy Peter's gift.[29] But Peter said to him, "Your money perishes with you, because you thought that the gift of God could be purchased with money!

In the Sermon on the Mount, Jesus preached to people's hearts. He wanted His audience to understand money's corrupting effects.[30] Money promises us much, but it demands even more. "Give me your heart," it says, "and I will save you."

---

[28] Matthew 6:19-20

[29] Acts 8:20-24

[30] Matthew 6:21

Its promises are without question among the greatest of Satan's lies. Money is a jealous god; it demands that we love it exclusively. Jesus concluded in this section of the Sermon on the Mount.

> *Matthew 6:24 (NKJV) 24 "No one can serve two masters; for either he will hate the one and love the other, or else he will be loyal to the one and despise the other. You cannot serve God and mammon.*

The hearts of the people have to be changed regarding money. Once their hearts are won, their practices will soon follow. The truth is people must be taught that riches can be deceitful. Money can be a major barrier to entering the Kingdom of God. We live in a society in which money is the primary, and for many people the only measure of personal worth. This is, of course, an absolute lie from the enemy. Our value is found in Christ and His work on the cross.

E.M. Bounds, reflecting on the deceitfulness of riches, said, "Few men get rich with clean hands. Fewer still get rich with religious hands. Fewer still hold on to their riches and hold on to Christ with a strong grasp at the same time."

John Wesley summed up his wise financial methods with his statement, "Make all you can, save all you can, and give all you can." In some places today the policy might be summed up, "Take all you can, spend all you can and borrow all you can."

Let us take a deeper look at Wesley's proposition. First, how can a person earn all he or she can. Scripture is full of advice and admonition on how to go about making all you can.

It usually comes down to diligence and integrity.[31] Society encourages us to make all we can, by cutting corners, get rich quick schemes, cheat, steal and get away with anything you can. We must continually remind our young people about diligence and integrity to counteract the influence of the world's propaganda regarding making money.

Wesley then advises people to save all you can. Scripture leaves no doubt that as believers we are to save.[32] People who save must resist the Western cultural values that encourage us to live for today, have it all now and live beyond your means.[33]

We cannot save if we owe others our future paychecks. Living debt free is one of the keys to discipleship, for the borrower is servant to the lender. When we build up consumer debt, we become slaves to those we owe, limiting our options to serve God fully.

People who live simply know the dangers of wealth and have learned to be content with what they have. When you receive a raise in your salary or unexpected inheritances, do you ask yourself, "What is the minimum I can live on, so I can save and invest in the kingdom of God?" [34] It is most important to save money for emergencies, retirement, and our children's education.[35]

---

[31] Proverbs 14:23; Jeremiah 17:11

[32] Proverbs 6:6; 21:20

[33] Luke 12:15

[34] Proverbs 30:7-9; Luke 3:14

[35] Proverbs 13:22

It isn't always possible to put aside adequate sums of money for these needs, but God will honor the small amount that we save, causing it to grow and making up for any lack.

There was a young couple leading our youth group, with a strong call to ministry. God had equipped them with the gifts and graces needed to lead and teach people to grow spiritually. He was in seminary and she was completing her master's degree in counseling. Upon graduation, they suddenly realized that their combined student loans prohibited them from entering fulltime pastoral ministry. As pastors, they would not be able to earn enough money to pay the loans off and pay for their living needs. As a result, they decided to take out more student loans, go back to school to earn doctoral degrees in counseling, and set up a private practice.

They are probably successful today because they were diligent and honest, but the kingdom of God may have lost something important because they were not free to follow their first love.

Wesley's third imperative is to give all you can. The world's motivation for investing is the accumulation of wealth for the purposes of personal power, pleasure, and security. In the Kingdom of God, we invest with a different goal in mind - that we may honor God.[36] If all we have is a gift from God, then the only wise investment is one that meets His approval.[37] God wants us to first invest His money in His Kingdom.

---

[36] 1 Corinthians 10:31

[37] 1 Corinthians 4:7

Christians need to understand, that their responsibility is to give generously to God's work. There is often a controversy about how much we are to give to God and how much we get to keep for ourselves. When Wesley died at the age of eighty eight he left a worn coat, a battered hat, a humble cottage, a tattered bible, the Methodist church, and an England that had been transformed.

God has entrusted the Church with much. Christian writer and leadership guru John Maxwell related this experience at a meeting a few years ago. One of his parishioners told him they were upset about what was happening in the church and as a result he was going to withhold his giving. Feigning shock, Maxwell stepped back quickly telling the shocked member, "You are robbing God and I don't want to be around if He decides to call lightning down upon you.[38]

If the ministry, church, or denomination is spending God's money wrongly, that is an issue between them and God. Our call from God is to give cheerfully. If one does not agree with the fellowship they are in, they are free to leave and meet elsewhere, but while they are in that group, they are called to give to that group.

Most Christians do not tithe. A few years back the average Christian gave approximately $145.00 per year. C. Peter Wagner, then head of the Fuller Institute for Church Growth, was a member of a very affluent church in Pasadena Ca. He writes, "...if all our members received California Welfare income, and tithed, our income would go up 40%.

---

[38] Stewardship Seminar

Jimmy Carter in 1975 had a taxable income of $122,189, yet his church giving was $6000.00 or 4.9%. Richard Nixon in 1969 gave $250.00 (or less than $5.00/week) to his church.[39]

R. G. Letourneau, the great Texas industrialist had the spiritual gift of giving. In his autobiography he said, "The question is not how much of my money I give to God, but rather how much of His money I keep." He turned over ninety percent of his company to his Christian foundation, and then he and his wife gave in cash ninety percent the income from their ten percent share of the business they kept.

Stanley Tam, who was in the silver business in Lima, Ohio, legally transferred fifty one percent of his company to his Christian foundation. He then gradually increased it to one hundred percent.

In his autobiography he said, "I frankly don't believe I'm as good a businessman as our financial statements indicate. I believe I operate far above my natural capacity."

There are basically two problems with people who do not give willingly; ownership and vision. People feel that they have earned the money. It is theirs.[40] In reality everything we have was given to us by God. He gave us the ability to earn money. Everything we have really belongs to Him.

---

[39] C. Peter Wagner, Your Spiritual Gifts Can grow Your Church.

[40] Deuteronomy 8:17-20

Vision may be the most significant issue in any stewardship campaign. There is always plenty of money and resources, but if the people cannot see vision they will not willingly support the ministry. They will want to become a part of something exciting.

Resources are not the problem. God does not need our money, He is wealthy.[41] But He wants us to realize He has given resources to us so that we can give to others.

It is natural for people to desire control over their finances. They feel that they have earned the money so it is theirs.

> *Deut. 8:17-20 You may say to yourself, "My power and the strength of my hands have produced this wealth for me." But remember the Lord your God, for it is he who gives you the ability to produce wealth, and so confirms his covenant, which he swore to your forefathers, as it is today.*

As leaders of churches and ministries your role in stewardship is not to ask for money. Your role is to share your dream for the ministry in a way that people want to become involved.

---

[41] Psalm 50:9-10

6. Submit to God

It was a clear day in San Diego's Mission Gorge area. The marine layer had burned off early and it was another beautiful day in paradise. My spirits were high and I was overflowing with the love of God. It was Monday, but very different than the rest of my Mondays at work. After returning from a men's retreat over the weekend, all I could do was bask in an afterglow of God's presence. The morning arrived too early, but lack of sleep could not destroy the sense of joy deep within me. Arriving at my company office late, most of the team had already left for their assignments. There were many routine items that needed my attention but nothing serious.

At lunch time I decided to take a leisurely walk down Mission Gorge to the Soup Plantation restaurant and get some soup and a salad. It is a buffet with a twenty foot long "build your own salad bar. Grabbing a tray and large salad platter, I fell into line behind two well dressed men having a rather animated conversation. They were obviously Christians because they were joyfully proclaiming the greatness of God and His work in their lives. They were talking between themselves but with a volume loud enough to be heard by each of the twenty or so people in line. I watched as they found a table over in a corner and selected a nearby table for myself so I could continue to share in their apparent joy in the Lord.

After the two men sat down and blessed their food, something suddenly changed. The loud joyful praise turned into a serious, subdued discussion and their countenance changed dramatically.

My desire to be near them disappeared and I wanted to crawl under the table and sneak away without being seen. But the Holy Spirit had other plans for me. He was about to teach me a great lesson that would take me several months to understand. It had to be a God thing because what followed was not possible in the natural. There was no voice or outward manifestation but deep within my spirit there was a sense as if the Lord said to me, "Pay attention, this is important, I want to teach you something."

My chair was about six feet from their table, behind and slightly to their right. One man was facing toward me, while the other had his back to me. It was then that I began to hear pieces of their conversation. When the man facing me spoke I did not hear a word he said. Conversely, I heard very clearly the words of the man with his back to me. It became clear to me that these men were pastors. The one whose back was to me was seeking counsel from the man facing me. The one facing me was there to help his friend. Hearing only one side of the congregation was strange but revealing. To this day, I can recite the exact words of two separate sentences spoken by the one with his back to me.

The first was, "I know now why my church is having so much trouble, the members do not submit to me as their pastor."

After more discussion he made his second memorable declaration, "The trouble with my family is the result of my wife not submitting to me as her husband."

Almost immediately, I sensed a different voice speaking to me from somewhere else, "This man is not submitted to Me." It was the Lord.

Fresh from a weekend of fellowshipping with Jesus and other spirit filled believers, I was ready for anything. Basically a shy person, I avoid confrontation whenever possible, but today, on this day, if the Lord directed me, I would go to that man, point my finger in his face, and declare, "You are having these problems because you are not submitted to God."

The Lord saved me from this total embarrassment with His next words, "No! I have showed you this for your benefit."

That incident was not the end of the lesson. It was the beginning of six months of being tested, beginning that very evening. When we get a new insight from the Lord or as He teaches us a new lesson, we like to share it with others. This was one I was anxious to share. At a home group meeting that night, a lady began to complain about her financial problems. This was not the first time. She had been having financial issues for years.

Armed with my noon time revelation, I felt compelled to share this insight with her. "You are having financial problems because you have not submitted your finances to God."

The woman's face turned purple with anger and my wife gave me a look that indicated I had committed the unpardonable sin. My statement may have been accurate but that was not the way or place to say it.

The meeting ended abruptly, but there was no escaping the woman's wrath. She was a neighbor and she was riding with us. It was a tense and quiet ride home that night. There were several more opportunities to give away my new insight and each time it failed to receive its intended respect.

Then one day, unexpectedly it hit me. Rita and I were driving up Balboa Avenue on our way to lunch when a light bulb lit up my mind. Slamming the dashboard with my right hand must have scared Rita, as I shouted, "I get it!" The lesson God had been trying to teach me was now clear. The enemy of our soul is able to attack us in the areas of our lives that we have not totally submitted to God. It is as if we are under God's umbrella of protection as long as He has control of our lives. But when we tell God that we would rather be in charge of things, He may back away and say, "Okay, go for it." That is where we get in trouble. As He lifts His umbrella of protection we are vulnerable to a spiritual attack.

Now I had to explain it to my wife, "Rita, when we suffer attacks from the enemy, where does he usually strike?"

"He attacks us in our finances." She replied.

"You know what that means don't you?"

"Yes, we have to cut up our credit cards."

That was not the specific answer I had in mind, but Rita is more detailed and logical while my response would have been more theoretical. We needed to put tighter restrictions on our finances, checking closer with the Lord when it came to expenditures.

At the time we were financially well off. My company was growing rapidly, we were receiving regular bonuses, and I had accrued sufficient vacation to accommodate our ministry activities. We maintained an attitude that it was our money and we would do with it what we felt was right.

We lived modestly, we gave generously of our finances to the church and other ministries, but we made most of our financial decisions without seeking the Lord's guidance. It was at that point we committed ourselves to submit to God in all of our financial dealings. Shortly thereafter, the Lord called me into full time ministry and since then we have relied on Him to provide for our needs.

Submission is a difficult concept for most people in our society today. The word itself evokes images of abuse and the sense of becoming a doormat. Yet both the Old and New Testaments tell us there will be great benefits when we submit to God.[42]

---

[42] Job 22:21; James 4:6-8

The word translated in the New Testament as "submission" means to place or arrange under. It is like products that are arranged on a display table or an army deployed to go into battle. It is also used to accept someone's admonition or advice. In our lives we often submit to our boss, the government, our spouse, pastor, or spiritual authority. We may also submit to our possessions, pride, and sin.

But the Bible instructs us to submit to God. Jesus Himself submitted to the Father. He did not do it from weakness but from strength. Our submission must be as Jesus modeled.

Submission is not becoming a doormat. Submission is more like an elevator. An elevator lifts things up. As we submit to God, we elevate Him. When we submit to our spouse we elevate him or her to a higher position. The purpose of submission is elevation or exaltation. As we submit to God, we exalt Him.

Jesus submitted to die for the church, to lift it up, to present it "In all its glory, having no spot or wrinkle, that she might be Holy and blameless. We submit to others to present them, in all their splendor, holy and blameless. The only way to lift people up is from a position of strength, not weakness. The entire basis of submission is not control but love.

There is a big difference between obedience and submission. You can obey without submitting. Children in their early years become easily bored in church. Our son would find all kinds of things to do on a Sunday morning sitting in church. It was a big distraction for his mother having to constantly tell him, "Don't do that."

He would obey and then find something else to do which would then cause more distraction and another rebuke. He was obeying, but he was not in submission.

We can be obedient in giving our time, presence, and resources to the church without being in submission. Scripture calls us to give to the work of the Lord. Therefore giving is obedience, but joyful giving and giving cheerfully is submission.

Submission pays big dividends. One simple illustration is our current vehicle. We dedicated it to God and have been using it for His service for over eight years. Awhile back, I realized the tires were showing a little wear and one had a very slow leak.

We rotated tires every other oil change and it had been a while since we had purchased any tires. It was time to buy a new set. Being curious, we asked the dealer to look up on his computer, the mileage the last time we bought tires.

We were amazed that we had over one hundred and twenty five thousand miles on that set of tires that had been guaranteed for only sixty thousand miles. We also got over two hundred thousand miles on spark plugs and brakes. These kinds of numbers are nearly impossible in the natural. God provided for the Jews as they wandered in the desert for forty years without their clothes or shoes wearing out so I guess He can extend the life of tires, brakes, and sparkplugs when we are submitted to Him.

7. Depend upon God

It was February 1991 a war was raging in the Middle East. "Operation Desert Storm" was about to end as US troops entered Iraq. A church in San Marcos, California was holding a renewal event a few miles outside the gate of Camp Pendleton, the headquarters for the 1st Marine Division. Most of the marines were overseas, but their families came to the church for spiritual strength. The area had been in a ten year draught with no sign of relief.

The bright sun reflected off the concrete pavement creating a mirage as we drove west on State Highway 178. My friend, Mylon Nelson, was at the wheel while I navigated from a map and written directions in my lap. We were on our way to visit a man and his sister whose illness had kept them from the meetings. Then it happened without any warning. This was many years ago and it is still a mystery. The manifestations were obvious, but what actually occurred is still a mystery. How and why it happened only God knows. For me, my life was changed forever. I went blind.

Without warning, the note, my hand, and the cars on the highway all dissolved in a pool of darkness. We were driving through the San Pasqual Valley, with the bright sunlight giving the world a golden glow, with no shadows or shade to be seen anywhere. One second, a brilliant countryside, the next second there was darkness. It was not total darkness. Straight ahead there was this large, black hole, a deep bottomless pit, surrounded by a ring of light around the periphery. At first there was a feeling of panic.

"What do we do now?"

Then a strange peace came over me and fear turned to curiosity.

"What just happened?"

Shutting my eyes and reopening them did not change anything. Closing one eye and opening the other alternately demonstrated the problem was in both eyes.

Mylon strongly suggested we head for the nearest hospital. But I felt our mission was more important. There would be time for the hospital later. We had an appointment to keep. Mylon would have to do his own navigating.

Twenty minutes later we arrived at our destination. Mylon took my hand and led me up the sidewalk, then rang the doorbell. A man opened the door, greeted us, and led down a dark hallway into a brightly lighted bedroom where his sister was lying in bed. Somewhere in the darkness between the doorway and the bedroom my sight returned.

"Wow! Was that weird or what?" It was at that point we realized that our host was himself sightless.

He explained he had lost his sight as he finished a round of golf. It happened suddenly. One minute he could see normally, the next he was sightless. He described a deep abyss surrounded by a small halo of light. His loss of sight had not seemed too traumatic for him. He sang in the church choir, and one of the other choir members would come and teach him the songs for week. It had led to a great relationship. We visited for awhile, and then prayed that God would heal his sight and his sister's ailment.

Thinking back on that day, it still does not make a lot of sense.

Did the Lord had give me insight into the man's condition by allowing me to experience what he had experienced, or had I suffered the same physical condition that he had and the Lord chose to heal me?

Theologically, it probably makes a difference, but to me, there was only one message; God is omnipotent. He is all powerful. In this life each one of us is vulnerable to sickness, injury, and death. The only way we can live free of fear is to depend upon God completely. It was that very same day that the war in Iraq ended and the draught was broken with the first of a long series of rainstorms.

People often make the mistake of isolating their spiritual lives from their secular lives. On Sunday, they enjoy a powerful church service, then get up on Monday morning and go to work thinking they now must get back to the real world. Church leaders often fall into this same trap. As spiritual leaders they will rely on scripture and the Holy Spirit to guide them, but when it comes to financial matters, they look for answers and guidance from the secular arena.

> *"... if the Holy Spirit were completely removed from the world today, 90% of the work of the church would go on as if nothing at all had happened." - [R.T. Kendell]*

With aging and dwindling congregations and an accompanying decline of finances main line denominations continue to close churches at an alarming rate. Leaders tend to blame their difficulties on the economy, the political situation or a younger generation that does not give as much as their parents.

The most common excuse we hear is, "There is too much competition." They cite competition from television, the internet, sports activities, and demands of career. They complain about spiritual competition from atheists, Muslims, Pagans and the New Age practitioners. Then there is the competition for the family's financial resources. Family income is down, prices are up, and jobs are scarce. All of these points are valid but they should not hold be holding back the growth of the Kingdom of God.

It was not like this in the church a few days after Pentecost.

> *Acts 2:42-47 (NKJV) And they continued steadfastly in the apostles' doctrine and fellowship, in the breaking of bread, and in prayers. Then fear came upon every soul, and many wonders and signs were done through the apostles. Now all who believed were together, and had all things in common, and sold their possessions and goods, and divided them among all, as anyone had need. So continuing daily with one accord in the temple, and breaking bread from house to house, they ate their food with gladness and simplicity of heart, praising God, and having favor with all the people. And the Lord added to the church daily those who were being saved.*

The early church had more poverty, more financial stress, and strong competition from the Jews, paganism, and adherents to Greek and Roman deities. The situation in Jerusalem was worse than what we face here in this country today. What was it about the early church that brought out the very best of the people?

After sitting in church board meetings for over thirty years, more often than not, we have realized that there is a disconnect between spiritual issues and "Church" issues. Spiritual issues can be resolved by depending upon God, but when it comes to financial and physical resources, too often God is ignored and dependence on man becomes the norm.

At leadership retreats we often ask attendees to select and prioritize their top five core values from a list of some fifty items. By far, "Depending upon God" is the most popular core value mentioned. But often it is only a theoretical value. It sounds good. It is the "Book" answer, but in practice it is often overlooked in favor of a more secular answer. We say we depend upon God, but in practice we put our faith in our personal abilities and worldly wisdom. Practically, many leaders become very nervous depending upon God. If they depend too much on God, then they are no longer in control. Control is a major problem in all organizations and the church is not immune.

Many people who claim to be Christians are "Functional Atheists." They believe God for their eternal resting place, but they live their lives as if God did not exist. They have fallen into the fallacy of believing that if you want something done right, do it yourself. They quote the imaginary scripture, "God helps those who help themselves." This is totally opposite to the teachings of scripture. When we are weak God can is strong[43]

---

[43] 2Corinthians 13:9

It had been an interesting week, our church finances were way down, and the leadership team had discussed various ways of stimulating the congregational giving. No decision had been made.

On Sunday morning before the service a young wife and mother came and asked if she could share a testimony in the morning service. We often encouraged members to share what the Lord is doing in their lives so it was not a big deal, but her testimony was. She did not have any idea about the leadership discussions nor the church's financial issues. It was a God thing.

This is roughly what she shared,

> *"My husband and I have been having an argument for the past year about tithing. He wants us to tithe and I could not see how it would be possible. I pay all the bills and there is not enough income to keep current, let alone give to the church. But he was insistent, so we started giving just a little each week. We have been tithing now for a couple of months and this is the first time we have had money left at the end of the month."*

She then continued, "I believe that this has been a turning point in our marriage. Now I know my husband is the spiritual leader in our family."

This blew us all away, that family had learned a lesson about obeying God and depending upon Him. But we also learned a lesson. God knew the needs of the church and was already at work to help us along.

Christianity Today's former senior editor Kenneth Kantzer described a conversation with a well known Korean pastor. He asked why, the pastor thought, the Korean church had flourished so magnificently in the last fifty years. The pastor responded,

> *"I think it is because we lived under severe Japanese persecution for so long. We learned to have no hope in ourselves but only in God. We learned to pray. We have been a suffering church and, therefore, a praying church.*

He then described his greatest fear for the Korean church,

> *"We are becoming more like you Americans. We are forgetting our suffering and our dependence on God. We are no longer poor in the things of this world. We are becoming wealthy and, our primary concern is how to get the good things of the world and how to enjoy them."*

Kantzer then writes,

> *"I can't exactly pray that God will make us suffer. But I can pray that we will come to realize our total dependence on God for what is best."*

How can leaders depend upon God in ministry and all aspects of the life of their ministry? The solution can be achieved by two specific changes in attitude. The first is ownership.

We often talk about "My Church" or "My ministry," when neither the church nor your ministry belongs to you. They are the property of God. He has merely given us a stewardship role over the day to day operations. According to the Parable of the Talents[44], we will be responsible for what we do with what we have been given.

As young teachers, my wife Rita and I developed a workshop on the infilling of the Holy Spirit for a Christian renewal conference in Southern California. The class went well and we were excited at the response.

After the session a layman from a San Diego church told us how much he enjoyed the class and felt it could help his church. He asked if we would share our notes with him so he could take it back to his church.

We were flattered and readily agreed. Later that day, a more senior teacher admonished us saying we should never give our teachings away, we should instead offer to come to his church and do the teaching. Chagrined we walked away, but something bothered us. It was not really our teaching. We put it together, but the Lord led us, through prayer, to put it all together. It was the Lord's. It came from a study of His word. It was not until much later that a wiser mentor advised us that whenever we gave something away, the Lord could give us something new. A serious mistake many church and ministry leaders make is to hold on to something too tightly. Sometimes we have to let go of something so that the Lord can give us something better.

---

[44] Matthew 25:14-30

Another change in attitude is a realization that God knows better than we do about our situation, and we can trust Him to be involved in the solution. After all, David pled with the Lord,[45] and depended on God. It requires us to trust Him and obey His direction.

Leaders will be able to depend upon God in financial matters when they read and follow His direction in His Word. In addition to His written word, God has provided us with the opportunity to seek His advice and guidance through prayer.

A San Diego church decided to seriously seek God's direction for the future of the church. A group of church leaders entered into a time of prayer and fasting culminating with an all-night corporate prayer session around the altar at the church. No one was to speak aloud, but was asked to write down on a sheet of paper what they felt the Lord was telling them about the direction for the church.

Each was free to leave at any time. Some stayed until after midnight others stayed until morning. Later when the papers were read, the notes all had a similar tone to the future direction of that church. The leaders now had a direction. Several years passed and nothing changed in the church. Why?

While God's direction was strong and very specific, inertia was stronger. The leaders failed to take action and obey God's specific direction. This is not uncommon, Jesus admonished His disciples, "The spirit is willing, but the flesh is weak."[46]

[45] Psalm 3:3-4

[46] Matthew 26:41

Not depending upon God is more an issue of apathy than it is of rebellion. If we are content with ourselves and our present circumstances we are less apt to follow God's direction if it requires moving out of our comfort zone.

In another church board meeting, the trustees were discussing how to finance the badly needed renovation of the parsonage. The small country church was having difficulty meeting current obligations let alone pay for the renovation. A grant from a family foundation had provided an initial ten percent of what would be required for the project.

Fund raising activities and Bank financing were discussed without agreement on a direction. An elderly trustee spoke up, "Just trust God. He will provide." This faith-filled utterance was acknowledged with only a few condescending smiles and one comment, "Let's get real." Others brought up Biblical concerns about borrowing money and being a servant to the lender.[47] The trustee spoke again, "If the Lord wants it built, He will provide." He went on to describe how the Lord had provided for the building of the Family Life Center years earlier.

Someone else spoke up, "Let's begin to pray for God to provide the resources and start a fundraising campaign and see what happens." That meeting and the prayers of the congregation initiated a series of "coincidences." The resulting renovation turned into a complete rebuild of the parsonage which was completed within nine months and the congregation did not have to borrow a dime.

---

[47] Proverbs 22:7

Coincidently a contractor began attending the church. Rather than lay off his workers when business was slow, he paid them out of his own pocket to work on the parsonage. The congregation raised enough money which added to the grant money paid for all required materials. An additional grant allowed for the purchase of modern appliances for the kitchen. There are no coincidences in God's Kingdom. The church depended upon God and God provided.

This did not stop them from doing all the things that constituted good stewardship of their resources and allowing their members to contribute to the effort.

Depending upon God does not relieve us of the responsibility to do the things that He wants us to accomplish. Jesus told His disciples that He only did what He saw the Father doing.[48]

Our tendency in church is to develop a plan, a program, or ministry based upon what we feel is important or needed. Just because something is good does not make it right for the church to be doing.

One of the best and safest ways to follow God is to discern what He is doing and then join Him in His ministry.

As an observer of ministries and leaders, the most painful thing to watch is a ministry or church that continues to try to operate after the Lord has passed them by. One of the church's problems is living on past glories, trying to recreate something that occurred years ago. Tradition has its value but we do not worship tradition, we worship a living Lord who is present and active in the world today.

[48] John 5:19

"The great sin of church not that we've lost power of God, but that we've become content to live without it." - [Charles Finney]

My fear is not that our great movement, known as the Methodists, will eventually cease to exist or one day die from the earth. My fear is that our people will become content to live without the fire, the power, the excitement, the supernatural element that makes us great. [John Wesley]

8. Motivation

It happened just the way the coach had told us while preparing for the big game against our rivals. The quarterback handed the football to the halfback started to run around right end. Our defense reacted and followed the ball carrier. Playing defensive end on the opposite side of the field, my coach's words stuck in my mind, "Don't be fooled, hold your ground, they will run a reverse." Taking two steps into the backfield, I stopped, watched, and waited. Sure enough, the halfback had given the ball off to the wide receiver on a reverse and he was coming straight at me. Everyone else had followed the halfback. We were the only ones on this side of the field. Holding my ground, he tried to run around me as I kept forcing him backwards and then tackled him for an eight yard loss. That day I probably played my best game and that single play was the highlight for me. The next day's sport's page featured an article on the game that finished with the line, "Johnson finally lived up to his potential."

"You have so much potential!" Those are the words often heard by many people. Those words are usually meant to be an encouragement but they are double edged sword. There is the positive; we have the potential to be successful, to grow, to become something great.

But there is the negative; we are not there yet, we are not as good as we think we are. Most of us never live up to our potential. Why do some people exceed their potential, while others with the same capabilities and same history spend their lives well short of their potential? Why is it that many people never realize their dreams and visions? The answer is motivation.

The church has done a reasonable job over the years of converting people to Christ, but has not been as successful in making lifelong, passionate, apprentices of Jesus. Our role here on earth is to follow and serve the Lord, accomplishing the tasks for which we were created, and becoming His people. When we face Him in heaven, we want to hear, "Well done faithful servant!" Not, "You had so much potential!"

Motivation is a reason or incentive to do something, a feeling of enthusiasm, interest, or commitment that makes somebody want to do something, or something that causes such a feeling. Motivation is what makes you keep going when things are tough.

The pastor of a medium size church in a nearby city confided in me, "I can't get the people to do anything. They just want to come on Sunday morning and be entertained." Since he had asked for our help, we decided to listen to the other side of the story. So without the pastor, we interviewed a few of his leadership team. We asked, "What do you think is the biggest problem with this church?" Each responded similarly, "The pastor won't let us do anything." This was not a single event. It has been a common response to the question. Pastors often blame their people and the people blame their pastor when things are not going right. It really does not matter who is right, what matters is the perception that one is right.

Leaders may be trying to motivate people, but may be demotivating instead. Motivation is the major issue in all leadership situations. How can leaders motivate their people to become more active? How can we motivate our people to give more of themselves and their resources toward expanding God's kingdom?

In the field of sports, it is not the most gifted player that makes the hall of fame. In business, it is not the smartest person that builds the largest company. In fact a study of CEO's of Fortune 500 companies indicates that most were "C" average students. Motivation is the major factor which will determine whether or not someone reaches their full potential.

As a leader, what motivates you to be great? What motivates you to lead? What motivates you to follow Jesus? If you are not motivated you may have a modicum of success but you will never reach your God-given destiny. You may have potential, but without motivation you will never fulfill God's plan for your life.

Our motivation can come from two separate directions. Extrinsic motivation comes from the outside; e.g. your mother threatens you with pain if you do not go to church or your boss gives you a raise if you do better on the job. Intrinsic motivation comes from the inside; the feeling of accomplishment, the satisfaction of helping someone. Intrinsic motivation just makes you feel good.

In his book, "Drive: The Surprising Truth About What Motivates Us," Daniel Pink[49] describes how traditional forms of motivation may, in some cases, decrease performance.

Pink cites studies conducted with college students in the USA and with villagers in central India. The results were consistent despite the obvious cultural differences.

The researchers found that as long as the task required only mechanical or routine performance, extrinsic rewards worked well. Higher pay given for higher performance yielded better performance. Reward and punishment motivated the people when they were required to just follow the rules. However, when the task became more complicated and required even a bit of conceptual or creative thinking, extrinsic rewards failed to motivate and even reduced levels of performance. Higher pay for solving puzzles, for creative thinking and for more complicated tasks had a negative effect on performance. Traditional (extrinsic) methods work well with small children, but as the children grow up these methods become counter productive. Other studies cited by Pink identified three major intrinsic factors which have the power to motivate individuals engaged in other than routine tasks; autonomy, mastery, and purpose.

[49] Pink, Daniel H. (2009-12-24). Drive: The Surprising Truth About What Motivates Us Riverhead Books Penguin Group

9. Autonomy

In 1979 we started a new division of an engineering services company in San Diego. As the company grew, new engineers were hired. Many leaders like to micromanage, it s a way of being in control. They must make sure people do what they told them to do and did it the way they wanted it done. In this model, employees are promoted and receive salary increases based upon how ell they follow orders. Using this hierarchal approach began to wane for me in about three months. A different approach would be necessary if we were to grow.

Delegation of responsibility and authority had always been difficult. But if we were to succeed, I had to get out of the way and allow my employees to take on more responsibility for their activities. I had to let go of my need to control. One of the first things I noticed was they did things differently than I would have done them. It took me a while to learn that once they were assigned a task, they had to be allowed to do it their way. These were thinking people doing technical jobs and my extrinsic motivational methods failed. So we hit on a new methodology. As each task was assigned, we would sit down with the project engineer, describe the project, discuss various approaches, and agree together on the direction to follow. The project engineer was then free to do it his way but he was still responsible for the accomplishment of the mission. At any time he could come back to me for whatever assistance he needed.

Giving your people autonomy may work in a business situation, but should it be used in the church or a Christian ministry? Autonomy is a strong motivator for most people today. They want to feel they have ownership over their life which allows them some control of their destiny.

In this post modern age, people are less likely to accept authoritarian leadership. Leadership may ask, "Isn't there the possibility of people getting confused by strange doctrines and get into bad practices?" Yes, there is that possibility but I believe one of the main problems holding the church back today is leaders who feel they must maintain control.

Jesus established a pattern when he gathered the twelve disciples. He taught them to minister with His words and by His demonstrations of spiritual power. He then gave them instructions and sent them out to minister.[50] Upon their return, they were debriefed and Jesus gave them further instruction. Jesus' practice was to train His followers, then release them into ministry, and then evaluate their efforts and give them further direction.

The apostle Paul was probably the most successful church planter of all time. Converted on the Damascus road in about 33 AD, his ministry lasted for approximately thirty years.

During that time Christianity, which began as a movement within the Jewish community in Israel, became predominantly a Gentile cult, at least in the eyes of the authorities of the Roman Empire.

---

[50] Luke 9 and 10

While Christianity arose among people whose language was primarily Aramaic, the foundation documents of Christianity have come down to us in Greek. Roland Allen writes that in one phase of his ministry,

> *"In a little more than ten years St. Paul established the Church in four provinces of the Empire, Galatia, Macedonia, Achaia and Asia. Before AD 47 there were no churches in these provinces; in AD 57 Paul could speak as if his work there was done, and could plan extensive tours into the far west without anxiety lest the churches which he had founded might perish in his absence for want of his guidance and support."*[51]

Using a team approach, Paul was able to delegate tasks and responsibility as his associates grew. Paul believed the church to be a group of people with specific spiritual gifts and graces, given by God.

He would identify a leader, lay hands on him to confirm the gift that God had given, and then Paul would move on to the next place God directed him to. In some towns Paul's stay was brief as the leaders developed quickly. This happened in Philippi where Luke was left to lead after only a short time.

---

[51]   Allen, Roland, Missionary Methods: St. Paul's or Ours, Eerdman's Publishing Co., Grand Rapids, 1962, page 3

At Berea, Paul left Silas and Timothy for a while until the church could sustain itself. In Corinth he stayed for a long time before heading for Ephesus with Priscilla and Aquila. Then he left them in Ephesus to help lead that church.

Each of us has a desire to be self directed. Traditional management techniques demand compliance. But if you want engagement, self direction is a better motivator. In his 1985 book "Unleashing the Church: Getting People Out of the Fortress and into Ministry,"[52] pastor Frank R. Tillapaugh, describes how his Denver church grew into a powerful outreach. When a member would come to him with a vision for a new ministry for the church, he would encourage the person to research what was available and put together a plan. Tillapaugh would then release them to lead the new ministry. He gave them autonomy.

Traditional leadership is based upon a hierarchal model which works well with routine, mechanical performance. The leader has authority by his position or title. Pastors who rely completely on their positional authority may function well in a legalistic organization but they will fail to motivate people to become true disciples, and this will often lead to spiritual abuse.

This is not the model of God's creation. Creation is based upon an orbital or relationship model. The universe consists of galaxies of stars; stars contain orbiting planets, planets, have orbiting moons.

---

[52] Tillapaugh, Frank R.Unleashing the Church,getting people out of the fortress into ministry, Regal Books, 1982, Ventura, CA

All matter is made up of molecules of atoms with electrons orbiting their nuclei. An orbital or relational model of leadership does not rely on positional authority but recognized authority. While this sounds radical to some traditionalists, it will yield a healthier following. Virginia Postrel[53] described the battle in our nation between "Stasists and Dynamists" that crosses all political lines.

A stasist enjoys things static while a dynamist likes dynamism. Stasists feel that controls must be placed upon all creativity and enterprise in order to eliminate mistakes. On the other hand, dynamists want see things change without restraints. Dynamists would rather step out into dangerous territory where they will make mistakes. Mistakes can be corrected, but the avoidance of mistakes by over controlling stifles creativity and progress. Dynamists ascribe to the "trial and error" process.

Postrel's point is that too much control will impede progress. One of the examples cited was the growth of the internet which had no controls and became the force that it is today because of its freedom. We have seen these phenomena in the Christian church where authoritarian leaders who hesitate to give their people authority and responsibility, will eventually see their ministries fail.

---

[53] The Future and its Enemies, The Growing Conflict Over Creativity, Enterprise, and Progress, Simon & Shuster, NY 1998

According to Dean Gilliland[54] a Methodist missionary to Nigeria in the nineteen sixties and seventies, the growth of the African church was inhibited for years by missionary leaders who refused to trust the native Africans to have any leadership roles. Roland Allen presented an alternative in 1927.[55] Citing Paul's success in Europe and Asia, Allen encouraged the church to release indigenous converts into ministry. Unfortunately Allen's words were not accepted until after his death in 1964, Today his books are required reading the Doctor of Ministry programs at major seminaries.

The pastor of a church will have positional authority based upon his or her appointment to a specific congregation. There are a number of ways this occurs. In the episcopal model of church government, the pastor is appointed to lead a church by an overseer or bishop who has authority over many churches. In the congregational model, the pastor is appointed to his position by the congregation who must approve of their leader. Some pastors and leaders gather their own groups and take on the senior position for themselves. Whatever form of government applies to your situation, you still have to rely upon the resources of time, creativity, and finances are supplied by volunteers.

---

[54] Gilliland, Dean S. Pauline Theology and Mission Practice, Albishar Bookshops (NIG) LTD. Plateau State, Nigeria, 1983

[55] Allen, Roland, The Spontaneous Expansion of the Church: And the Causes Which Hinder It. First Published 1927, Now available through Jawbone Digital http://www.JawboneDigital.com

As a result a relational model of leadership is more effective than the more traditional authoritarian model. The relational model will serve to motivate people to creatively work together for the spiritual and physical growth of the church. Over - critical and authoritarian pastors and leaders often find they have no followers. They have to learn to allow some degree of autonomy, in their followers. When members of a body feel that they have a degree of autonomy and are able to provide input, they are more willing to participate and contribute their resources, time, and creativity.

10. Mastery

In the fifth grade our daughter Rhonda was an average student, working hard in school. Like most pre-teens it was difficult to get her up in the morning to go off to school. Then one day she came home and announced she wanted to play the flute in the school band. Up until then she had no musical ambitions that we knew about other than dancing classes. As she continued her flute lessons, her whole attitude toward school and life changed. She attended a band camp at William & Mary College in Virginia and continued to master her music. Now that she has grown children of her own who are musicians she continues to enjoy playing and dancing.

There are thousands of amateur musicians who practice daily and sometimes play gigs on weekends. Why do they do it? It does not support them. They do it because it is fun and the challenge of mastering their craft. Mastery is the urge to improve ourselves. It does not matter whether it is playing an instrument, teaching a class, or digging a ditch. Human beings have this deep-seated desire to master something. Motivation to work harder comes from the desire to become excellent at something. The most discouraging words you can hear from someone are, "I am no good at anything."

Humanistic psychologist Abraham Maslow published an article in "Psychological Review" in 1942 [56] proposing that humans strive for an upper level of capabilities. They seek the frontiers of creativity, the highest reaches of consciousness and wisdom. This has been labeled a "fully functioning person", "healthy personality", or as Maslow calls this level, "self-actualizing person."

Maslow set up a hierarchy of five levels of basic needs: Physiological needs; Safety needs; Need for love, affection, and belonging; Needs for esteem; and Need for self-actualization. Maslow describes self-actualization as a person's need to be and do that which the person was "born to do." "A musician must make music, an artist must paint, and a poet must write."

One of the saddest expressions to hear in church is, "I am not being fed." There can be many meanings to this statement. It can mean simply that the pastor does not cater to their whims, they do not feel a sense of belonging, or their felt needs are not being met. It may also mean that they are not growing spiritually. We have to acknowledge here that there are probably more church members who do not want to grow spiritually, than those who hunger for more. Unfortunately leaders often cater to the former and leave the latter hungry. So they spend their time and money attending conferences and supporting televangelists.

---

[56] *A Theory of Human Motivation* (originally published in *Psychological Review*, 1943, Vol. 50 #4, pp. 370–396).

As a Christian there is one thing that is important for us to master; being a disciple of Jesus Christ. The Greek word for disciple is mathetes. In ancient Greece a mathetes was an individual that attached himself to teacher or leader in order to learn from him. We would call this an apprentice. If one wants to become an electrician, he looks around and finds a master electrician under whom he can train. The apprentice attaches himself to the master electrician and follows him around day in and day out until he then becomes a master electrician. Jesus commanded His followers to go and disciple all nations, teaching them everything Jesus taught His followers.

The leader's task is to strive for excellence in following Jesus and teach your followers to grow and learn everything that you have been taught. The church must provide for its people opportunities to grow spiritually and learn the deeper things of God. The writer of the letter to the Hebrews gives a strong admonition to get going and get growing.[57]

---

[57] Hebrews 5:12, 13

11. Purpose

Moses did not merely lead the children of Israel out of the slavery of Pharaoh's Egypt just to escape the harshness and bitterness of life there. He had a driving vision that propelled him to lead approximately two million people through the wilderness of perils, obstacles, and interim defeats to a place they could actually see ("vision") in their mind's eye, "a land flowing with milk and honey." Getting to the Promised Land was Moses' governing, long-term purpose. It was such a distinct, attractive, and compelling purpose that it drew his people, as if attracted by a powerful magnet, through enormous difficulties toward one all-attracting goal. Moses is a good study of the process of realizing purpose, he never reached the Promised Land himself, but he lived his purpose for the last third of his life.

Nehemiah realized his God given purpose when he restored the walls of Jerusalem and brought honor back to the nation. Identifying a purpose for your church or ministry should not be approached in a frivolous manner. When observing successful people, it is easy to see that, one way or the other; many have been driven by a very clear, compelling personal sense of purpose.

Several years ago a church consulting organization compiled the results of questionnaires they had given to over two thousand protestant churches. In the survey, given to every church member, they were to rate their church's effectiveness in twenty-seven different categories.

The categories included; worship, evangelism, music, fellowship, preaching, stewardship, etc. The consultant then compared responses from each church and with the rate of growth or decline of that church's attendance. If a church was growing rapidly it would be interesting to see what they thought they were doing right. The most significant factor across all growing churches would certainly be useful. High on the list for church growth were, preaching, worship, prayer, and evangelism. But the most significant factor affecting numerical growth of the church was having a clear, focused, God-given purpose. It topped evangelism by four percentage points.

Clear Focused Purpose

A search of scripture will demonstrate that there are two basic reasons that the church exists in the world today; (1) edification - encouraging, equipping, strengthening and nurturing of its members and (2) expanding the kingdom of God - making disciples of all peoples. These are general reasons, and they are both massive in scope. Every single church or ministry has a part in fulfilling these biblical mandates for the church. The specific purpose of each ministry is unique to that body based upon its gifts, graces, and environment. Therefore its clear focused purpose cannot just be a motto that fits on a logo. It must be specific for their abilities and their environment. A clear, focused, God given purpose must answer three specific questions: Who am I? Why am I here? Where am I going? It must be determined through intense prayer allowing God to provide His input.

Who am I?

Several years ago I was invited to minister at an area meeting of pastors who shared the same spiritual DNA. There had been a restructuring of their leadership and many were confused as to the direction of the new leadership team. They had been comfortable with the previous administration but unclear about the new team. They had felt a loss of their identity. Organizations as well as individuals must have an identity. At my suggestion they began to share the things which were of prime importance to them as individuals. Much about who we are revolves around the things that are most valuable to us. Value is a concept that describes the beliefs of an individual, culture or an organization. A set of values may be placed into the notion of a value system. Values are considered subjective and vary across people and cultures. Types of values include ethical/moral values, doctrinal/ideological (political, religious) values, social values, and aesthetic values. Personal values guide decisions by allowing for an individual's choices to be compared to each choice's associated values. Personal values developed early in life may be resistant to change. They may be derived from those of particular groups or systems, such as culture, religion, and political party. However, personal values are not universal; one's genes, family, nation, and historical environment help determine one's personal values. Each individual possesses a unique conception of their own values, i.e. a personal knowledge of the appropriate values for their own genes, feelings, and experience.

Groups, societies, or cultures have values that are largely shared by their members. Members take part in a culture even if each member's personal values do not entirely agree with some of the normative values sanctioned in the culture. This reflects an individual's ability to synthesize and extract aspects valuable to them from the multiple subcultures to which they belong. If a group member expresses a value that is in serious conflict with the group's norms, the group's authority may carry out various ways of encouraging conformity or stigmatizing the non-conforming behavior of its members. For example, imprisonment can result from conflict with social norms that have been established as law.

In addition to identifying our value system, it is important to understand our unique set of gifts and graces. Aslan Ministries[58] has a free resource for identifying the spiritual gifts identified in Romans 12:6-8 which will help you identify your specific gift mix.

Why am I here?

The question is really two questions which must be answered; why me and why here? As you look around your city, or the environment of your ministry, ask God, "Why me and why here?"

Lynne and Tom were appointed to a church in an urban neighborhood near Los Angeles.

---

[58] www.aslanministries.org

As the community changed over the years, most of the aging congregation moved to the suburbs, and a mostly Latino population moved into the surrounding area.

Those that moved out retained their membership and loyally drove several miles back for services in their church. With an aging and dwindling congregation and a backdrop of a growing Hispanic community, Lynne and Tom asked themselves, "Why are we here?"

Tom's gifting was in the area of evangelism while Lynne had teaching and leadership gifts. It did not take long for them to realize that the future of that church lay in the reaching out to the surrounding community. When they explained to the membership that they had two choices; continue to shrink as members passed away and eventually shut the doors or they could reach out to the community with the Gospel of Christ and bring them into their church. The membership agreed to become a ministry to the community. As a result they were able to fulfill their unique purpose because they asked the question, "Why are we here?" Jesus knew why He came to earth. He presented His purpose in the synagogue in His hometown of Nazareth.

> *"The Spirit of the Lord is on me, because he has anointed me to preach good news to the poor. He has sent me to proclaim freedom for the prisoners and recovery of sight for the blind, to release the oppressed, to proclaim the year of the Lord's favor."* [59]

---

[59] Luke 4:18-19

Where am I going?

At a meeting in California, we were reacquainted with a classmate from seminary who was planting a church in Colorado. Things had been going well for him, so we asked him to share his story. We had been involved in the successful planting of two churches and were starting on our third which was growing very slowly. He explained that the first thing he did upon arriving in town was to set aside two weeks of prayer and fasting in order to hear the Lord for direction. Sometimes in our busy-ness we attack a situation using our own ideas and our own strengths instead of seeking God's direction. His plan excited me. As soon as we returned home we entered into fourteen days of prayer and fasting. On the thirteenth day of the fast, just as we had settled into bed, the phone rang. It was a pastor we knew in Louisiana. He was planning to leave his church to plant a new church in another city and asked if we would be interested in taking his church. We had no desire to move as we were already planting a church in Mississippi, but we had been seeking the Lord for direction and maybe this was our answer. When we told him we would pray about it, he invited us to come over to meet with them and discuss the situation. Then we were torn between what we doing and what we could do in Louisiana. We contacted a friend and advisor and asked him to pray about the situation for us and let us know what he senses. He then gave me some very sage advice. He said, "Do not move unless you get a vision for the church and its ministry." To find out where you and your ministry are going, you must have vision.

12. Vision

A Sunday school teacher once told her class, "When it is dark tonight, go into your back yard and count the stars." The next Sunday kids reported their counts; the first kid reported seeing a million, another saw fifty thousand, another five hundred. Then one kid proudly announced. "I counted twenty seven stars." He then explained to the rest of the class, "We have a very small back yard."

The Declaration of Independence was passed by the Continental Congress on July 4, 1776, and announced that the thirteen American colonies, then at war with Great Britain, regarded themselves as independent states and no longer a part of the British Empire. On that day in England, the King of England, King George, wrote in his diary," Nothing important happened today." Our ability to see is not just with the eyes. Helen Keller was asked, "What could be worse than being blind?" She Replied "Having sight but not seeing." Vision is the ability to see beyond our limitations, beyond the size of our back yard.

According to John Maxwell[60], vision requires four elements; (1) the ability to see, (2) the faith to believe, (3) the courage to do, (4) and the hope to endure.

---

[60] INJOY Life Club Volume 4, Lesson 10

The Ability to See,

The "ability to see" is our awareness of our environment, what is going on around us in both the physical world and in the Spiritual world. King George was like the kid in the Sunday school class who had a small back yard. Many of us suffer from a tunnel vision. We are unable to see beyond our fences. If you truly want to realize God's destiny for you, you will have to work hard to increase your awareness. We cannot limit the possibilities to what we can see in the visible world. We must learn how to listen to the Holy Spirit, seek the Lord, and spend time at His feet. Many of us are so busy doing many things that we do not spend enough time just being with Jesus. We are like Martha who needed to learn to be more like Mary.[61] We cannot limit ourselves to just the audible and the logical.

> *Psalm 121:1-2 I lift up my eyes to the hills, where does my help come from? My help comes from the Lord, the Maker of heaven and earth.*

The Faith to Believe

Vision requires faith. Without faith, it is impossible to please God.[62] We must believe that we can do all things through God Who strengthens us. Believing requires faith. Can you see yourself writing a great novel, painting a fine painting, or winning people for Christ?

---

[61] Luke 10:41-42

[62] Hebrews 11:6

Do you have faith to create great things, to accomplish great things? Jesus said, "According to your faith will it be done to you."[63] This is the "Faith Factor." Faith is a gift from God. But faith requires some action. You can believe that a man can push a wheel barrow across Niagara Falls on a tight wire, but faith is required to get in the wheelbarrow and be pushed across the falls.

The Courage to Do

Faith requires action. It takes courage to be used by God. Joshua had the courage to step out in faith and to cross the Jordan River into the Promised Land. God gave him a huge task leading an entire nation into a hostile land and taking the land for God. There is a relationship between the size of the cause and the size of your courage. Courage rises when the cause is greater than our circumstances. The cause of gaining the Promised Land far exceeded the circumstances of wandering around in the desert for forty years. Courage falls when the circumstances are greater than the cause; therefore our cause must be great. The cause we fight for is to rescue people from the grip of Satan and lead them into a relationship with Christ.

There is no greater task. There is a cosmic war going on for the souls of humankind and we have been called to be soldiers in that war.

Our flesh encourages us to live in our comfort zone – God encourages us to live in the courageous zone.

---

[63] Matt 9:29

Courage begins with fighting battles over our own character, self-discipline and will. Plato said the first and best victory is to conquer self. Pogo said, "We have found the enemy, and it is us." Our biggest obstacle is ourselves.

The Hope to endure

"I have fought the good fight, I have finished the race, I have kept the faith."[64]

To endure means to hold up under fire. To endure is to have the ability to withstand hardship, adversity, or stress; to remain firm under difficulty, without yielding. Winston Churchill wrote, "The nose of the bulldog is slanted backward so he can breathe without letting go." Cotton Mather, a famous Puritan pastor prayed for revival every day for twenty years.

As he was on his death bed, the First Great Awakening began. So often we have the tendency to give up when the going is tough. We may think that God is closing doors and that we may be going in the wrong direction. It may be that the circumstances are bigger than our cause, but sometimes we just get tired and our faith begins to wane.

---

[64] 2 Timothy 4:7

However, this is the time to realize that the Lord may be testing us. Are we serious about following Him? Is He really leading us? James, the brother of Jesus tells us: "Blessed is the man who perseveres under trial, because when he has stood the test, he will receive the crown of life that God has promised to those who love him."[65]

---

[65] James 1:12

13. Get a Fresh Vision

A couple of dozen pastors, evangelists, and ministers of evangelical churches gathered for a small conference at a mountain park a few miles outside San Jose, Costa Rica. They had come to learn how to be more effective in making disciples of Jesus Christ in their nation. The North American leader of the conference had prepared several hours of teaching focused on revitalizing ministry and developing leadership skills. As the group slowly gathered, the speaker was led to throw away his agenda, notes, and expectations. The Costa Rican church leaders were coming as a last resort. They had been struggling for years in difficult ministries with little fruit to show for their efforts. They were completely exhausted and frustrated from ministries which had yielded little fruit. The conference leadership changed the agenda from a teaching meeting to a ministry time for the local pastors and leaders. First, there was a time of intimate and serious worship of the Lord, then a time of prayer ministry for each of the wounded attendees. The conference ended with a five minute message. The message was, "Get a fresh vision from God for your ministry. If you don't have a fresh, clear vision of God's call, get out of ministry and go sit at the Lord's feet until you receive that fresh vision."

As we realize our own limitations and see the needs around us, it is easy to become despondent.

There is so much to do, and we are so weak, but we are only tools used by God to accomplish His purpose in the world and we serve a very big God. He is omnipotent. It is in our weakness that He is strong.

> *I can do all things through Christ who strengthens me.* [66]

Seeing beyond our limitations creates enthusiasm, defines boundaries, produces effort, unites us, and rallies us. God will give you a fresh vision of His purpose which will re - energize and excite you. Our tendency when seeking a vision for our ministry is to look at ourselves and our own capabilities. But if you want to find out what the Lord has in store for your ministry, do not look to yourself, look to God. If you have been struggling to find your God given purpose, you probably need a fresh vision from God.

Before we can get a fresh vision <u>from</u> God, we will have to get a fresh vision <u>of</u> God. We may want to see Him in a new light. Peter went fishing in the wrong place at the wrong time because Jesus' directed him to. As a result, he saw Jesus in a new light and had a new vision.[67]

Out in the Midian Desert, Moses was tending livestock when God called from a burning bush. He had a fresh vision of God and discovered his call.[68]

Isaiah saw God, and was forever changed."[69]

---

[66] Philippians 4:13

[67] Luke 5

[68] Exodus 3:10-12

These men received a fresh vision of God, and then received their call and their destiny was realized. We all regularly need a fresh vision of God. This can only come as our relationship with the Lord grows deeper. If you want to receive a fresh vision from God, follow the pattern of Isaiah: Worship, Confession of sin, Forgiveness, and Service.

We need a fresh vision of God's Holiness

"Holy, holy, holy is the LORD Almighty; the whole earth is full of his glory."[70]

Isaiah was in the temple worshipping when he received a fresh vision of God. It was a vision of God's holiness, "Holy, holy, holy is the LORD Almighty; the whole earth is full of his glory." John, the beloved apostle, received a new vision of God's holiness.[71] Holiness refers to God's nature. Holiness means we have to believe that God is always right. We may not understand, but at the deepest part of our being, we know that He is right.

We cannot judge God. In this life we only see partly, but when we see Him face to face, we will understand.[72] We need to repent of judging God and realize His holiness.

---

[69] Isaiah 6:1-9

[70] Isaiah 6:3

[71] Revelation 4:8

[72] 1 Corinthians 13:12

There has been a move in much of the church to place God on a human level, so that we might more easily understand His love. In the process we tend to lose the awesomeness and holiness of God. When the angels repeat, "Holy, Holy, Holy," it shows the completeness of His holiness. He alone is supremely holy.

We need a vision of our own sinfulness.

"Woe to me!" I cried. "I am ruined! For I am a man of unclean lips,

In the presence of God's holiness, Isaiah realizes his own sinfulness. This is a direct consequence of being in the presence of holiness. The closer we get to the holy God, the more obvious our lack of holiness becomes. We must always be hungry for more of God, and be humble before his awesomeness. We must become teachable, able to take correction. There is no room for ego or pride. It is not "what a great thing I am doing for God." We have to be in touch with our own sinfulness.

"and I live among a people of unclean lips,"

We need a vision of the condition of this world. Isaiah knew the sinfulness of the world in which he lived. As we come closer to God and His holiness, we begin to understand the sinfulness of the world around us. At times we forget how far from God the world has gone. We look around and begin to compare what is happening now with what happened in the past several years and think this is normal.

Our normal is what God calls unclean. We have been like the proverbial frog in the kettle that is unaware of the water getting hotter and hotter. Suddenly when it is too late, the frog is cooked. In the presence of the almighty and holy God, we see what needs to be changed. Even though Isaiah knows that the world is loved by God, as we should, Isaiah also knows that the world is headed for disaster.

We need a fresh vision of the power of God's word

> *Then one of the seraphs flew to me with a live coal in his hand, which he had taken with tongs from the altar. With it he touched my mouth and said, "See, this has touched your lips; your guilt is taken away and your sin atoned for."*

We need a fresh vision of the power of the word of God. As we look around at this sinful world, the task of bringing about change appears to be so great that it is impossible. Faced with an impossible situation, there are normally two possible actions for us to take. "Type A" personalities will jump in and begin to do everything because there is so much to do. This does not work. Within a short time this individual will suffer burn out, possibly get ill, and lose his effectiveness. Others will look at the situation, agree that it is impossible, and sit back and do nothing. There is a third option. This is the one which will accomplish the Lord's purpose and bring peace to the individual.

Believe that the word of God has the power to save.[73] Believe that the Lord has a role for you in His solution to the problems of the world. Find that purpose, and fulfill it.

God will provide the purification[74] [75] for the world just as He does for Isaiah as we admit our sinfulness and humble ourselves before Him. God has the power to transform the world.

We need a fresh vision of our own potential.

"Here am I. Send me!"

In spite of our sinfulness and weakness, we can do all things through Christ, who strengthens us. We have enormous potential when we are walking in God's calling. We do not get to define that call. We cannot just go do something, and ask God to bless it. The call must come from God, and then we respond. We do not determine the size of our task; we say, "Here I am, send me."

"A task without a Vision is drudgery,

A Vision without a task is but a dream,

A Vision with a task can change the world."

[Anonymous]

---

[73] Romans 1:16

[74] Numbers 31:22-23

[75] Malachi 3:2

14. Communicate

Leading a ministry is a hundred times easier when the leader is able to communicate with his team, his constituents, and the people he desires to impact. There are three things you must communicate: your vision for the ministry which will include where you want to go, what will it looks like, the benefits of achieving the vision; where you are today, your progress in accomplishing your vision, successes and weaknesses, any road blocks or problems which must be overcome, and concerns you may have about reaching your goals; and third you must communicate new goals, direction and strategies for achieving the vision.

John Wimber gave a group of church planters seven "Constants" for building a church.[76] The first two were constantly tell your story and constantly tell His story. As a leader gathers people to his ministry he is to constantly communicate what he wants to accomplish, his vision, and how God has brought him to this point. Nehemiah shared his vision of Jerusalem's reputation being restored by rebuilding its walls and how God was behind the plan.[77]

---

[76] Church Planting Seminar, February, 1993 Anaheim Vineyard

[77] Nehemiah 2:17, 18

Leaders must be able to communicate a vision so clear that their supporters can see it in their mind's eye. The vision must be clear and the benefits of achieving it must be significant. When supporters can share the vision, they will be motivated to support the leader and his vision.

Most building programs are supported because they are easily envisioned. Members can see the vision. There will be drawings to look at, models set up in the lobby, bricks and mortar that can be touched, or there is an old building in disrepair. Motivation is more difficult for a new outreach ministry or discipleship program. Good leaders communicate, clearly, fully and regularly. Nehemiah found out that a group of people can lose sight of the vision in just thirty days. It is well for the leader to restate and recast the vision at least once every month.

One of the most important items the leader must communicate regularly is his vision for the ministry. Supporters or potential supporters of a ministry or a special fund drive must believe that they will be supporting something important. Nehemiah arrived at Jerusalem and told no one why he was there until he could assess the situation.[78] After his midnight inspection, he called the elders together and cast the vision of a restored Jerusalem with its walls intact. The city would no longer be ridiculed by its neighbors.

---

[78] Nehemiah Chapter 2

He told them of his plans to rebuild the walls and how God was in on it. When they heard all this they caught the vision and enthusiastically agreed to follow him in this significant project. Nehemiah, in a single sentence, told them the situation they were in, he gave them an action statement and gave them a vision of a better future.[79] This motivated the Jerusalem elders in Jerusalem to join in the effort to rebuild the walls. Their purpose statement contained current condition, action, and results. He assured them that God would lead them and strengthen them.[80]

A generic purpose statement that states, "We will make disciples." does not evoke images in people's minds. It only evokes questions, "What is a disciple?" "How are we going to accomplish this?" "Where will we find the people we will disciple?" A clear focused purpose is specific; it defines a context, an action required, and the results to be realized. If you want people to be involved and contribute time, resources, and ideas to the ministry you lead, they must be motivated by the importance of the work.

People have to believe that what they are doing has a purpose, is important, and has significance. As Christian leaders the cause of Christ is the most important thing in which we can be involved. There is a battle raging for the souls of men, women, and children and we are involved in that battle. Our purpose is always to expand the kingdom of God and rescue the perishing.

---

[79] Nehemiah 2:17

[80] Nehemiah 2:18

As we considered a move from Mississippi to Louisiana to accept the pastorate of a recent church plant where the founding pastor was leaving, a mentor offered me some sound advice, "Do not move unless the Lord gives you a vision for that church and the community." We waited and did not make a hasty decision. We were in the process of starting a church in Mississippi and were not going to leave unless it was the Lord's will. Then about a month later, driving home from lunch with a prospective leader for our fledgling church the Lord began to show me how the Louisiana church could affect its community. That night, as our living room became a place of worship, I realized that it was time to move, and prayed that my wife Rita and our small group would understand. That same day Rita had felt a peace about our move to Louisiana. Our first three years in that church were difficult because of unresolved issues from the previous leadership, but that our vision, received that day in Mississippi while driving home from the lunch, was strong enough to keep us on track. The vision included an outreach to the relationally broken, a place for healing of the whole person, a separate service and facility for youth and young adults, and churches of the community uniting for the betterment of the entire city.

Vision is not always cast in concrete, it is a dynamic thing a situations change. After the first three years things changed and the church began to fulfill its role in the community and live up to vision we had when we arrived. When that happened we revisited our purpose statement. The original purpose read:

Our purpose is to experience God's manifest presence through Biblically based worship, teaching and loving relationships; resulting in passionate, faithful, fruitful followers of Jesus Christ who depend upon God, are led by His Spirit, and extend His love throughout this area and the world..

We then changed it to:

Our purpose is to provide opportunities for people to experience the presence of God; resulting in passionate, faithful, fruitful followers of Jesus Christ who depend upon God, are led by His Spirit, and extend His love throughout this area and the world

The change was an admission that we could not change people. Only God can change people's hearts. But we, the church, can provide opportunities for people to experience God and then Jesus can change them. The leader cannot be the Holy Spirit to those who follow.

In addition to restating the vision on a regular basis, it is also important to communicate the present situation. There are some who cast a vision which is so ambiguous or so far reaching that it may never be achieved. A good vision is one that can be measured and progress can be charted. People must be informed regularly of the current status of the organization and how well it is progressing toward its purpose. A program with a visible structure is easy for one to measure.

Jerusalem's walls were visible to Nehemiah and the people. They could see the progress. After thirty days when progress became stalled, Nehemiah could point out the problem and make corrections. A fund raising effort with the thermometer chart measures progress. There may be some leaders who share good news with enthusiasm, but withhold anything negative. This is often experienced where church finances are concerned. In one church with financial problems they began to put a giving report in the weekly bulletin compared with the required budget amount. When this failed to motivate greater giving, they decided to remove the bulletin information because, "it was too embarrassing."

Two churches had the identical problem. One, a down town church, had a fairly large budget. Over the span of a few years some members had left for jobs in other cities while a few others moved to other churches. The falling attendance meant a decreasing income.

The budget was reduced reflecting the reduced income, but they were still spending more than was coming in using up their surplus from previous years. The declining income was posted in the Sunday bulletin for all to see, but nothing changed. The pastor preached on stewardship with no success. The finance committee reluctantly decided to write a letter to the congregation laying out the situation and requesting the membership review their giving and determine whether they could give more.

The letter worked, people responded with the comment, "We did not know it was that bad or we would have given more." They did not get it by reading the bulletin notes. They did not get it when the preacher talked about stewardship. They did get it when they were able to read it in a letter. This resolved their financial situation.

The second church was a rural church with a stable attendance. Spending had continued to rise to the point where they were spending more than they were receiving in offerings. They also needed to renovate their parsonage. Similarly, they were reluctant to relate the whole story about their financial situation. Finally they wrote a letter to the membership similar to that of the first church, with similar success. When the church membership or ministry followers understand the true situation they are willing to support the needs.

The third item that needs to be communicated regularly is how we are going to get to the next goal as we move toward achieving our vision. As progress moves ahead or stalls their may be changes in how we move forward.

When the enemies of Jerusalem threatened to attack and the men working on the wall were getting tired, Nehemiah reorganized his team and posted half his men as armed guards so the other half of the men could work without fear.

The enemy saw that God was still with the Jews and they left them alone. Our plans change, so we must be flexible to respond to changing situations and keep everybody informed as plans change.

Too often a situation change calls for a quick response from leadership. When leaders fail to communicate what and why they are changing course, people feel left out of the decision process.

15. Be Generous.

Earlier we stated that people will follow leaders. They will emulate the leader's attitudes and practices. If you want your people to grow spiritually, you must be growing yourself, if you want your people to trust and depend upon God you must go first, and if you want them to be generous with their time and resources, you must be generous with yours. It will not work to preach about giving if you yourself are not a giver. This is difficult to accept by some leaders because they are afraid that generosity with their time will be taken advantage of by demanding people. Grant[81] explains that there are two kinds of "Givers." There is the "selfless" giver who is often taken advantage of by others. He is a super candidate for early burn out. He will also have a difficult time completing his own work and will often be passed over for promotion. After committing myself to the Lord, I could never say no to anyone who asked me to take on a new assignment in the church nor had a need. Rita was the same. We both were "Type A" personalities, always on the go. But soon we both began to run dry and burn out. It was Rita who first learned to say, "No!" It took me a lot longer. Then there is the "otherish" giver who thrives while helping others to achieve their goals while still working effectively. The "otherish" giver has been shown to be more successful than the takers or matchers who have similar positions. While "selfless" givers

---

[81] Grant Ph.D., Adam M. (2013-04-09). Give and Take: A Revolutionary Approach to Success Penguin Group US.

give without regard to their own needs, "otherish" givers consider their own time and efforts important but are always willing to help others. Before a commercial airliner takes off we hear the cabin attendant make the obligatory gas mask announcement. They always conclude with a statement appropriate to givers, "If you are assisting someone else with their gasmask, put your mask on first, and then assist your fellow passenger." That has to be the approach you use in your generosity.

Grant explains,

> *"By and large, because of their tendencies toward powerful speech and claiming credit, successful takers tend to dominate the spotlight. But if you start paying attention to reciprocity styles in your own workplace, I have a hunch that you'll discover plenty of givers achieving the success to which you aspire."[82]*

Back when we first learned about the spiritual gifts described in Romans 12, I felt it would be cool to have the gift of giving and have money to give away. Earlier we had dedicated our company and career to God and He had led us to a place of relative comfort. So I prayed and asked the Lord to give me the gift of giving. The bible does tell us to seek spiritual gifts.[83] The Lord answered my prayers. Looking back now from a more mature perspective, I am not sure whether or not that was a wise request. With that particular gift there <u>was a burden of respon</u>sibility. As financial bonuses and

---

[82] Grant Ph.D., Adam M. (2013-04-09). Give and Take: A Revolutionary Approach to Success (p. 255). Penguin Group US.

[83] 1 Corinthians 14:1

salary increases came in we learned to ask, "Why, what is this to be used for?" We were never able to keep much for ourselves. If we were too slow in giving it away, the car would break down or the house would need repairs or something unforeseen would require the money.

Since our model for effective leadership is Jesus we should look at His generosity. Paul writes that Jesus was rich but became poor that we may become rich.[84] Before He walked this earth, Jesus lived with all the riches and splendor of the ivory palaces of heaven. He was surrounded constantly by the glory and power and majesty of the Father. Then he came to earth in the womb of Mary. Jesus lived His earthly life as a poor man. He was not a destitute beggar, yet, He could say of Himself "Foxes have holes and birds of the air have nests, but the Son of Man has nowhere to lay His head."[85] Most amazing of all is why Jesus accepted this simple life of poverty: This was Jesus' "giving." He gave financially in the sense that He accepted a humble life of poverty when He had all power to live as the wealthiest man in all history, and He did it for our sakes. Why would Jesus need to become poor for our sakes? It demonstrates to us the giving heart of God. It shows us the relative importance of material things. It gave others the privilege of giving to Jesus.

Jesus was an "otherish" giver. He regularly took time away from the crowds and from His disciples to pray and dialogue with the Father. He only did the things that the

---

[84] 2 Corinthians 8:9

[85] Matthew 8:20

Father told Him to do. While seeing to the needs of others, He maintained boundaries which allowed Him thrive.

The task of a spiritual leader is to assist others to becoming the people God created them to be. It is the leader's job to sacrifice his desire for the people in favor of God's desire for the people.

John Wesley's model bears repeating here; earn all you can, give all you can, and save all you can.

16. Six Steps to Financial Health

Ministries and churches are supported voluntarily by people who have a relationship to the ministry. While scripture, doctrine, and membership vows compel people to support their local church with time, resources, and presence, each person must make his or her own decision as to what that means. As a leader it is your responsibility to grow a healthy ministry.

Churches and Christian ministries are organic in nature, that is, they are made up of people rather than equipment, brick, and mortar. When living organisms are healthy, they grow. When they lack health they tend to dry up and die. The financial health of a ministry will be enhanced when the leadership maintains a model of integrity and generosity while casting a worthy vision. The vision cannot be based alone upon the capabilities of the leadership, but must include the intervention of the Lord in order for it to succeed.

There are six steps to financial health for any Christian ministry.

1. <u>Submit to God.</u>

First the leader must be in submission to God. When leaders are intent upon their own agendas, they crowd out the Lord's agenda. Too often pastors and leaders try to please their constituency in an effort to maintain their support. As a result they hesitate to speak the truth in love for fear of losing support.

Autonomy is a strong motivator, but leaders who desire authority must themselves be under authority. We can not have complete autonomy and still submit to God. Either He is in control or we are.

God will protect what belongs to Him, but we are not assured that He will protect us if we fail to elevate Him to that position of authority. We cannot be sure that His umbrella of protection extends over what does not belong to Him. The Bible tells us that our obedience to Jesus will result in fruitfulness.[86] Christianity is not just about following certain rules; it is about following the Ruler. In the kingdom of God, He is the Ruler.

2. Depend upon God.

Depending on God is similar but not identical to submitting to Him. When we depend upon Him, we realize that it is not in our own strength but in His strength that we depend.

By depending upon Him, we do not limit our vision to the things we can easily accomplish. Depending upon God opens the doors to all kinds of successes. There are some who might misuse this concept and sit and wait for God to move. Depending upon God requires obedience on our part to what we already know we are to do.

---

[86] John 15

3. <u>Motivate People</u>.

A leader has to be a good motivator. Each individual is motivated by slightly different methods. A good leader knows how to motivate individuals as well as the group.

4. <u>Communicate</u>.

We have heard pastors make the comment, "What if they do not agree with my vision, they might leave?" If people do not share the vision of the ministry they should be allowed to leave rather than stay and fight for their agenda. When people are not of the same mind regarding direction of the church or ministry, they would be happier somewhere else.

When ministries fail, most fail because the leader does not communicate effectively. Communication includes written correspondence, electronic messages, social media, and verbal face-to-face meetings. It is important to realize that just because it was announced in the morning service and it was included in the bulletin, does not mean the people heard. Information needs to be communicated often and in different modes.

When flying on an airplane, the important safety information is announced and also contained on a card in the seat pocket, but some never get the message. Enterprising flight attendants do some weird things to get the point across.

A good leader communicates three things regularly; his vision for the ministry, the status of the ministry at that point, and the future goals of the ministry.

5. Be generous.

Whatever a leader wants his followers to become, he must become first. When the leader is generous with his time, finances and knowledge, his followers will become more generous with their time, finances, and knowledge.

According to Adam Grant studies show that generosity is contagious. When people are treated generously, they are more inclined to be generous to others. People who received from others increased their giving to others. Scripture tells us that there are also many personal benefits to being generous.

6. Maintain an Attitude of Gratitude.

Doctors say the healthiest emotion you can have is gratitude. It is the absolutely healthiest emotion you can have. In fact the more you work on this attitude of being grateful, the healthier you will be. Be thankful for everything you receive. Each day find five things you are thankful for and express your gratitude to God.

Acknowledgements

We would like to acknowledge Ron and Rebecca Bounds for their ministry of support of many ministries but especially for their love, prayers, and encouragement to us. We would also acknowledge the support of the Aslan Ministries Board of Directors; Ron and Rebecca Bounds, Bruce and Elaine Wimberley, Larry and Natalie Dautenhahn, and Beth Wynn. Additional thanks go to Beth for her editing of the manuscript of this book. We would also like to acknowledge those who have led and taught us along the way: Rev Dave Walker for his gentle encouragement and exhortation; Rev.'s Larry and Audrey Eddings who mentored us in leading ministries; Rev. Don Guerrant for his energy and willingness to foment change in the church and people; Gary Georgeson for his willingness to speak the truth into my life even when it did not feel good, and for being a pastor to us.

We also owe a debt of gratitude to the late John Wimber for model he gave us of being willing to follow the Lord where ever He leads.

We also want to acknowledge all of the people who have attended our classes throughout the world for their continued friendship and for what they have taught us.